In Awe of the Ordinary

In Awe of the Ordinary

C. Welton Gaddy

BROADMAN PRESS
Nashville, Tennessee

© Copyright 1977 • Broadman Press
All rights reserved.
4282-49 (BRP)
4251-51
ISBN: 0-8054-5151-X

Dewey Decimal Classification: 248.4
Subject headings: CHRISTIAN LIFE

All Scripture quotations, unless otherwise indicated, are from the Revised Standard Version.
Scripture quotations marked KJV are from the King James Version.

Library of Congress Catalog Card Number: 76-50951
Printed in the United States of America

*To
Judy,
John Paul,
and
James Welton*
(three extraordinary people)

Preface

For most persons, the Christian pilgrimage is pursued amid familiar surroundings and in relation to friendly acquaintances. Faith pervades a common routine as it finds expression in ordinary tasks. Witness occurs in office suites, along factory assembly lines, in telephone conversations, and everywhere people meet to buy and sell, visit, recreate, and take care of the business of life. Prayers are silently uttered while people run to and from engagements, while they wait at a traffic light, and while they strain to remain calm amid the mounting pressures of an average day.

Unfortunately, the impression is sometimes given that Christianity is only special when occasions for testimony or demands on behavior are special. Holiness is equated with detachment from the normal, large projects rather than small tasks, and unique experiences rather than common events. So, questions are raised: Is the greatness of the Christian faith recognizable and attainable to persons caught up in meeting day-to-day responsibilities? Can an individual experience the breadth and depth of holiness in the unglamorous routines of life as well as in dramatic circumstances? Such questions receive positive answers as the false equation of unholy with ordinary is refuted in this book.

Motivated by the truths of the Bible, informed by personal experience, and refined in dialogue with fellow believers, the words on the following pages affirm the sufficiency of the Christian faith for all situations. The common stuff of life is described as the scenario for an encounter with "the holy." No traumatic crises or spectacular demands are discussed. Temptations are recognized. Challenges provoked by seemingly mundane ministries are considered. The abundant resourcefulness of personal faith is explored. Together these reflections on the Christian life constitute a statement of belief that the ordinary is precisely the realm in which Christ intended for redemptive faith to be practiced and his personal presence to be experienced.

Obvious but too important to go unstated is the author's indebtedness to the many mentors of these thoughts—college and seminary professors whose ideas have been confronted in the classrooms in which they taught, and in the books which they wrote; acquaintances kind enough to share in long conversations and articulate enough to state their views in a systematic manner; and other friends capable of communicating the profundity of their beliefs only through their attitudes, spirits, and general behavior. Gratitude marks each encounter with these persons' contributions of truth.

Many of the materials in this volume were originally shared through sermons, lectures, and informal discussions. Additional reflection and writing related to the thoughts have arisen within a fulfilling ministry with the Christian Life Commission of the Southern Baptist Convention. The process of preparing these ideas for publication has frequently and happily been interrupted by questions and comments from John Paul and James Welton, sons whom my wife and I believe to be extraordinary, telephone conversations with friends and associates, meetings in both our church and community, and numerous other legitimate and rewarding demands for time and attention. As usual, my wife Judy has been the one who helped me keep my priorities in order, my personal relationships nurtured, and my work done without a sacrifice of love.

Emphasis in this volume is upon the good news of the Christian message. No individual need despair over the ordinariness of the days or the persistence of recurring responsibilities—here is where God may be met. These words are offered with the prayerful hope that they may encourage gratitude for the gift of the holy and nurture sensitivity to the grace which pervades all of life.

C. Welton Gaddy

Contents

1. The Sanctity Of The Ordinary 17
2. Living In The Now 26
3. The Blessing Of Inconveniences 37
4. The Danger Of The Commonplace 48
5. The Privilege Of Temptation 60
6. Costly Grace 73
7. Christianity In Work Clothes.............. 86
8. The Atheist Within 95
9. The Near Ends Of God...................106
10. For Everything A Season 118
   Notes 126

Earth's crammed with heaven,
And every common bush afire with God;
But only he who sees, takes off his shoes,
The rest sit round it and pluck blackberries.
                        ELIZABETH BARRETT BROWNING

The Sanctity Of The Ordinary

"My father, if the prophet had commanded you to do some great thing, would you not have done it? How much rather, then, when he says to you, 'Wash, and be clean?'"

2 Kings 5:13

"Nothing will sustain you more potently than the power to recognize in your humdrum routine, as perhaps it may be thought, the true poetry of life—the poetry of the commonplace, of the ordinary man, of the plain, toil-worn woman with their loves and their joys, their sorrows and their griefs."

SIR WILLIAM OSLER

1
The Sanctity Of The Ordinary

Does the ordinariness of things ever bother you? The same activities which you have been involved in for months confront you with future demands and no prospects for change are evident. Everyday engagements begin to take on the characteristics of patterns which threaten to become hard and fast routines or perhaps even ruts. Persons caught up in this syndrome, who really try to fight it, tend to lose themselves either in serious plans or fanciful daydreams. They concentrate on something different—doing something really big, being a part of something really special.

Christians are not immune to such a temperament of character. In fact, it is the struggle of many who move from involvement in every aspect of a local church program to a passive relationship to any body of believers. These people begin to reel under the weight imposed by an uncreative routine which at one time had been viewed as holy tradition. Uncritical introspection produces thoughts which interact in such a way as to form a rationale for doing nothing rather than doing the same old things again. Positions of responsibility within the fellowship which once seemed glamorous and challenging slip so much into the realm of the ordinary that they are not attractive.

Ecclesiastical program planners seem particularly adept at recognizing this tendency in people. The result is denominational calendars filled with special emphases. In an effort to prevent any individual from falling into a practice of ministry which can be considered ordinary, special days, weeks, and years are planned. The problem is not solved, though. Once the special event is over—once the celebrated day has ended, once the revival has come and gone—ordinary acts seem even more ordinary. The flame that appeared to burn so brightly during the big event is almost snuffed out in an environment of demands for ordinary acts of service.

Here is both the plight and the challenge of the Christian faith. It is in the realm of the ordinary, not outside of it, that believers most thoroughly work out their salvation. Faith is most clearly demonstrated in a person's ability to do the little things, the small acts, the ordinary duties.

The biblical account concerning Naaman's experience with Elisha (2 Kings 5:8–14) makes the point in a delightful way. Naaman was an important person, commander of the Syrian army, "a mighty man of valor," but a man suffering from the dreaded disease of leprosy. When, with some difficulty, he came to meet Elisha, the prophet of God, and asked for help, he was insulted by the ordinariness of Elisha's reaction. Naaman wanted to be healed. But, he felt in order for healing to occur he would have to be welcomed royally, prayed over loudly, and treated spectacularly. Elisha did not even greet the man personally. Moreover, the healing methodology prescribed by the prophet was far from spectacular. Naaman was told to go and wash seven times in the Jordan River.

The leper from Syria became so indignant that he almost missed the opportunity to be healed. A hasty retreat on his part was prevented by the helpful insight and therapeutic advice of his servants. These wise and faithful laborers reminded their leader that it was just as important for him to do this ordinary thing as it was to do something he considered really special. Naaman saw the truth. Realizing that he would have readily followed a daring command which required great courage, this important military man agreed to participate in a seemingly small and insignificant exercise. Notice carefully. It was in doing that which was little, ordinary, and apparently unimportant that Naaman found healing.

What a parable of the entirety of the Christian life! Whether one opens the pages of the Bible to the Old Testament or to the New Testament, God is found sanctifying ordinary acts. Biblical history revolves around ordinary events which for the people involved took on deeper meaning other than what was obvious on the surface. Ordinary acts are filled with deep spiritual significance.

One of the problems people had in relation to Jesus was a hesitancy to entrust to him the cherished title of Messiah and the costly commitment of their lives to such an ordinary individual. Surely, many of his contemporaries must have at least thought what one leading character dares to sing in a recent Broadway musical about Jesus—"He's a man, he's just a man."

Fellow citizens of Nazareth found their familiarity with Jesus to be a stumbling block to belief. Read their conversation: "Where did this man get this wisdom and these mighty works? Is not this the carpenter's son? Is not his mother called Mary? And are not his brothers James and Joseph and Simon and Judas? And are not all his sisters with us? Where then did this man get all this?" (Matt. 13:54–56, RSV). The problem with these people was that they could not conceive of God working through one whom they knew so well, an ordinary resident in the community.

Neighboring villagers also had difficulties with their belief. They inquired of each other, "Can anything good come out of Nazareth?" (John 1:46). How unlikely it seemed that God would reveal himself through one who had lived in such an ordinary little village.

Ordinary acts, by far, characterized Jesus' ministry. True, he did work miracles. However, Jesus did not emphasize the miraculous. Consistent with other components of his ministry, miracles were only a means of service, even if made unusual in nature because of the special needs of people in trouble.

Jesus made significant the common process of teaching and learning—not through extraordinary educational techniques but through periods of dialogue which occurred on a mountainside, in a boat, along a busy road, and in scores of other familiar places. Who had not seen the towels with which slaves washed the feet of house guests? Yet, Jesus took such a towel and made it the symbol of fellowship and servanthood as he used it to wash his disciples' feet. Roman crosses dotted the landscape frequently. However, it was the use of such a cross in the ordinary procedure of crucifixion which became a way of salvation when Christ was the crucified one.

More clearly in Jesus than anywhere else or in anyone else it is obvious how God sanctifies the ordinary. What is learned from Jesus' actions is further enhanced by his teachings. The Lord's instructions to his disciples always lie within the realm of the possible, of the ordinary. To assist individual believers in an understanding of their tasks, Jesus told about persons who possessed only one talent. And he gave sanctity to the one act an individual may be able to do well. Additionally, Jesus told about a sower who in doing his work met with failure as well as success. Not expecting anyone to be 100 percent effective in every endeavor, Jesus gave meaning to all work.

Consider what Jesus asks of his followers, what he expects

The Sanctity Of The Ordinary

of his disciples. At every point the action desired is within the believer's grasp, perhaps even so common a responsibility as to be called ordinary. Jesus requests that people get straight in their hearts the matters of ultimate loyalty and belief. Every individual deals with this issue daily. Decisions are constantly being made regarding to what or to whom people will give themselves, and in what or in whom individuals will place their faith. Jesus merely injects himself into such deliberations and challenges persons to find life's greatest value in serving him. Thus, the ordinary acts of personal belief and self-giving are sanctified and endowed with eternal importance.

But how is Christ to be served? Surely this must be the point at which Christians are ushered into realms of responsibility far beyond the ordinary. Study closely the kind of behavior Jesus expected of his disciples. There were to be those disciplines of self-examination when believers looked at themselves under the revelatory light of prayer, scriptural study, church teachings, and the like. Also, Christians were to engage in acts of ministry aimed at helping others.

Jesus was very specific in stating his intentions for Christian ministry. A true disciple was depicted as one who would give hungry folks food, thirsty people drink, strangers welcome, naked individuals clothes, sick persons visitation, prisoners concern, unloved people love, penitent persons forgiveness, enemies prayers, and a church supportive involvement. As Matthew 25:31–46 makes clear, Jesus equated faithful discipleship with such ordinary acts of service that those involved were amazed at the significance inherent in what they had done (or failed to do).

What makes the difference? What is it that gives sanctity to an ordinary act? How is it that one person can sit and eat with friends finding no unusual joy in the experience while another can participate in a common fellowship meal and be filled spiritually as well as physically? Why is it true that one individual can meet someone in need, sensitively assess the situation, facilitate helpful responses, and feel spiritually uplifted while another engages in the same activities and only feels bothered by additional responsibilities?

The ordinary act is sanctified when it grows out of obedient faith in Christ and when it is offered as service to Christ and in his name. That which seems so simple and unimportant takes on the significance of a kingdom event when done for Christ and in his name!

The problem is that many believers have never seen or felt the sanctity of the ordinary act. Most everyone stands ready to do a big deed. Call on people and they will participate in the spectacular. Challenge folks and they will placard the work of the church before the entire community. Strangely enough, when people feel that what they are doing is really special the activity seems all the more holy. The impression is misleading, however.

The whole thrust of biblical truth is that there is as much holiness in the ordinary as in the spectacular, as much commitment in the small act as in the large. Some individuals spend their time waiting for the really big thing to come along and attract their attention when what is most needed is a reassessment of their willingness to serve Christ in ordinary events—teaching a class, leading a study group, rearing children, offering forgiveness, sharing a meal, giving a tithe, working for a good home, attempting reconciliation, making oneself available to the needs of a local church, deepening personal faith.

Enhanced by the light of the New Testament witness, consider again the suggestion from Naaman's servants. From the lips of ordinary individuals with extraordinary insight, here is helpful advice for every Christian. "If you were asked to do something great, wouldn't you do it?" they asked. "How much more willing you should be then to do a small thing. For it is in the ordinary that you may experience the greatest depths of sanctity." The servants were right.

Christians must nurture a sensitivity to the sanctity of the ordinary. Otherwise, some of the richest opportunities for spiritual growth and ministry will be missed. After all, who would ever have thought to look in an ordinary cattle crib, or on an ordinary Roman cross, or beside a common tomb to find the Savior of the world! Who would have expected that Jesus Christ, the Son of Almighty God, would spend his days on earth among the blind, the lame, and the lost or that he would hold up as religiously significant the use of a loaf of bread, a towel, and a cup of cold water! Who would ever have dreamed that the long-awaited Messiah involved in the redemption of the world would have had time for a little child to sit on his knee and be loved by him! Who would ever have thought it!

Living In The Now

"When Jesus saw him and knew that he had been lying there a long time, he said to him, 'Do you want to be healed?'"

John 5:6

*"Tomorrow—oh, 'twill never be,
If we should live a thousand years!
Our time is all today, today."*

JAMES MONTGOMERY

2
Living In The Now

Our home phone rang. The voice on the other end of the line was strangely familiar but unrecognizable. Finally, the caller identified himself. Dear friends from college days had recently moved to town. Immediately, we made plans for our families to be together. After our first visit we scheduled others. Real joy was derived from reminiscing about school activities in which we had been involved and updating information on mutual friends. After several outings with this couple, my wife observed that all of our conversations and fellowship had been built around the past. She remarked, "I am ready to get to the present and the future."

A young married couple came to me asking for counseling. Their problem was a fascinating one. A few weeks earlier they had attended a meeting in which the focus of attention was the second coming of Christ. Assuming insights and authority that not even Jesus could claim, program personalities had pinpointed the imminent end of history and dated the second coming. Exploiting the unknown, various speakers voiced gory threats as well as glorious promises regarding this period of time. Though the husband expressed only minor interest in such concerns, the wife was completely enthralled by thoughts of the rapture, the end of time, and the millennium. She grasped at meanings far more speculative than biblical. Apocalyptic literature had become her only testament.

The husband wanted a child and said so. As a response, the wife piously quoted Mark 13:17 ("And alas for those who are with child and for those who give suck in those days!"). Applying to herself words intended for the residents of first-century Jerusalem, she warned her husband that all thoughts of a child had to be delayed. Both people needed help. Their marriage was severely troubled by the wife's preoccupation with the future.

Placed side by side, these two experiences dramatize the significance of a proper perspective on both the past and the future for a healthy present. Development of that kind of posture receives encouragement and assistance from various biblical writers.

Addressing himself to the Corinthian church (2 Cor. 6:2–10), the apostle Paul reminded the Christians there of their responsibility as ambassadors for Christ. He challenged them to exhibit in the present the fruits of that redemptive experience which was theirs in the past. Underscoring the importance of a daily witness, Paul warned the Corinthian Christians that without such actional testimony, contemporary associates could judge their former acceptance of God's grace to have been in vain.

Another emphasis is present in Paul's words to these people. The great missionary quoted directly from the prophecy of Isaiah 49:8 and then announced the arrival of the very time which Isaiah had anticipated. Paul's message was, "Promise has become fulfillment. The long-awaited day of salvation is at hand. You are now living in that day. God has acted decisively in history. The Messiah has come. Salvation is available. So, today you are to respond. You are commissioned as messengers of this good news and the most opportune moment for your ministry is now."

Notice that the foundation as well as the realm of application for both of Paul's emphases—an elaboration of what God is doing and an accent on what God's people are to do—is in the present. Consider the apostle's words: Behold, *now* is the accepted time; Behold, *now* is the day of salvation (2 Cor. 6:2, KJV). In the now, in the present, is where Christ is to be accepted, where faith is to be exercised, where biblical morality is to be practiced, where ministry is to be done, where the breadth, width, and depth of the Christian life is to be experienced. Christian discipleship demands living in the now.

A person who is free in Christ is free to live for Christ in the present moment. A person without such freedom is enslaved and in exile.

To live entirely in the past or in the future is to live in exile.

Much growth is stunted and many lives are stifled as persons wrap around themselves the heavy chains of tradition and invest the entirety of their lives in the past. You have heard or perhaps participated in the revelatory chants of this disposition—

"I just wish I could regain that feeling of security which I had when I was a child."

"Let's return to the days when religion soothed and never troubled, when morality was simplistic instead of complex, and when ministry focused only on individuals rather than on individuals and structures."

"Before my spouse's death I never experienced trouble."

"Life will never again be as good as it was when I was younger."

Please do not misunderstand. The past cannot be dismissed lightly. The past *is* important, very important. That which lies behind us is extremely significant as our informer and teacher. Experiences from another day become guideposts helping us better to understand where we are going and providing us with points of reference by which we can measure how far we have traveled. However, when the past takes on so much importance that a person lives more in memory of yesterday than in awareness of today, there is trouble.

Memory can be deceptive because it frequently acts selectively. Thus, for a person in exile, mental safaris into the past may be either sentimental journeys or horrifying excursions.

Sometimes nostalgia takes over. Troubles are forgotten as good experiences are singled out and idolized. The conviction develops that nothing can ever equal the joy of those recalled moments. Persons with such a perspective become victims of the past rather than free agents capable, with God's help, of responding to what is happening in the present. They need to be jarred out of a joy based entirely in another day so they can come alive in the present and experience happiness today.

Conversely, memory may blot out all positive experiences and enforce a preoccupation with that which is bad. Minor mistakes, broken relationships, and moral failures so dominate reflections on the past that no consideration is given to previous accomplishments, fellowship, and integrity. Persons enslaved to such a torture chamber-like past desperately need to hear the words of grace and forgiveness which open the doors to the present and offers the opportunity for new life now.

A cafeteria experience from elementary school days instructed me in the danger of concentrating on the past. I was returning my lunch tray to the counter while looking back over my shoulder at the table where I had been seated. Suddenly I felt a bump and everything on the tray began to rattle. I looked ahead. There in my path stood the principal of the school. Appearing very provoked and seeming to stare right through me, she snapped, "You had better read about Lot's wife!" Well, I was relieved. What I had expected was a much worse fate. That admonition did not mean much to me until I discovered that the life of Lot's wife came to a fearful and abrupt end because of her desire to look back to the past rather than to perceive the present. The profundity of the good principal's remark was obvious.

A major problem among those people so integrally involved in the crucifixion of Christ was their commitment to the past. They were so captivated by a religion of tradition and principles of another day, that they were blind to what God was doing in their very midst. Informed by ancient writings and satisfied with the way things had always been done, they wanted no alterations in their sabbath observance, no changes in their services of worship, and no new emphases in their legalistic code of morality. Because Christ, the radically new revelation of God, did not fit neatly into one of their tradition-informed and rigidly-constructed mental categories, they rejected him. So in bondage to the past were these people, that they continued to affirm what God had previously done but refused to accept what the same God was presently doing. The exile finally took its tragic toll. "Religious" people crucified in the present the very God whom they were willing to praise as long as he remained in the past.

Both individuals and churches must beware of the crippling bondage inflicted by such a past-oriented approach to life. Symptoms of its pervasive reality are evident in confessions of inflexibility—

"I have never done that before and I am not going to start now!"

"Who ever heard of that taking place in days gone by?"

"We have always done this the same way."

To live only in the past or to adopt a life-style of looking back is not only to choose exile, it is to invite danger.

Pain may be involved, but it is absolutely essential that disciples of Christ be sensitive to God's summons to the present and be willing to serve him today. Jesus Christ the liberator frees his followers from the past and empowers each of them to live for him in the present.

Just as people may be in exile with the years of the past forming the boundaries of their bondage, so may they be enslaved to the future. Some individuals give themselves to the future with such completeness that their lives become almost meaningless in the present. In fact, it is very easy to idealize tomorrow in a manner that makes life seem to hold little significance today.

Most persons who harbor glorified views of the future spend the present in endless waiting. No doubt you have heard or perhaps participated in their litany of restlessness—

"I will become a Christian just as soon as . . . ."

"Once I am out of school, I will get my life-style more in line with Christian morals."

"When I am married and the parent of a child I will feel more like a real human being."

"Our church should take on that ministry when . . . ."

Some of the Christians in the church at Thessalonica had become obsessed with the doctrine of Christ's second coming. Their only activity in the present was to ponder the future. Paul confronted them with the stern reminder that such abject idleness constitutes sin (2 Thess. 3:6–12).

A dominant futuristic orientation to life adversely affects almost every sector of a person's existence. Present commitments and involvements are rendered tentative by grandiose visions of a tomorrow which is expected to dawn momentarily. Interpersonal relationships are weakened. An individual in bondage to the future seldom accepts other people for who they are. Friendship is extended on the basis of who acquaintances could be, will be, or might become. Thus, people preoccupied with the future dehumanize others by denying them the right to be themselves in the present.

Discussions of the future are perfectly in order. Such deliberations, whether in regard to persons or institutions, are healthy, necessary, and legitimate. However, constructive plans for the future which grow out of present involvements must not lure us into a debilitating bondage to the future which renders us ineffective now. The future is not to be the time of the disciple's greatest ministry. Today is that time.

If to live entirely in the past or in the future is to live in exile, to live in the present is to be at home with Christ.

The Christ who came to proclaim "release to the captives" calls all people out of exile—whether in relation to the past or to the future—and welcomes us home to the present. This is "homecoming"[1] for the Christian—coming alive to the present and accepting the challenge to live life to the fullest now. It is also an experience of grace—God granting to us the courage to be at home in the now when it would be much easier to retreat to the past or escape into the future. Certainly it is the realization of freedom—memory and expectation retaining places of importance but losing their binding power as chains. Every person can experience God now—not just as others have experienced him in the past, not just as some had hoped to experience him someday in the future, but now!

With Christ we can enter into the present knowing that this moment is just as significant as any past or any future.

Now is the time for shouldering new responsibilities, embarking upon new pilgrimages, establishing new relationships, firming up new commitments. No one need wait any longer for things to be as they were or for situations to exist as they could be. A person's only opportunity to experience the ideal is within the humdrum moments of the present.

Consider carefully Jesus' encounter with the lame man by the pool of Beth-zatha (John 5:1–9). Ponder Jesus' question to this sick man: "Do you want to be healed?" At first these words seem unusually cruel.[2]

Jesus dealt with a man who had been in the same place for thirty-eight years. In exile both to the past and to the future, this poor individual rationalized his situation in terms of both lamentation and anticipation—"I've been here thirty-eight years and nothing has happened. Somebody always beats me into the healing waters. Oh, but one day I will reach the pool when the water is troubled and I will be healed." Jesus challenged the man to forget the past and the future and to confront the now—"If you want healing, why not today? This moment either take up your bed and walk or be sick!" The decision had to be made immediately.

In reality, we are never merely on the verge of anything.[3] The present moment reveals that we are either doing something or we are not. Those who delay major decisions and redemptive involvements while waiting for a more opportune moment, better conditions, or a more inspirational feeling must realize that God's judgment assesses us in terms of who we are and where we are in the present.

Admittedly, some people do not want to be a part of anything which they do not originate. These individuals desire either to be the whole show or have no role in it. However, life is simply not like that. Only rarely, if ever, are individuals privileged to be involved at the very inception of something. For the most part, life is lived out in the middle.

A past always precedes us and the promise of a future is ever before us. Yet, that is as it should be. The present is our home and the ordinary our environment. This is where Christ may be most redemptively met. This is where Christ may be most helpfully served.

Exile, in the sense of bondage to the past or to the future, is always chosen. People decide to live in yesterday or tomorrow for various reasons. However, no one has to choose exile. All may choose freedom. The good news of the gospel is "You can be free!" Today is the day of new beginnings.

Christ stands ready to help any individual come home to the present and offers to live with all of us here and now. How true the Bible is—"Behold, *now* is the acceptable time; behold, *now* is the day of salvation" (2 Cor. 6:2).

The Blessing Of Inconveniences

"One day while Moses was taking care of the sheep and goats . . . the angel of the Lord appeared to him as a flame coming from the middle of a bush."

Exodus 3:1–2 (TEV)

"The good things of life are not to be had singly, but come to us with a mixture."

CHARLES LAMB

3
The Blessing Of Inconveniences

Why do things always seem to happen at the wrong time? Why is it that some of the most demanding situations arise when one least expects them? No one is exempt from periodic intrusions by the phenomenon of the inconvenient.

You have the proverbial million things to do. A friend, upon whom you have relied on numerous occasions, requests your assistance in a worthy project. It is a necessity that you give a positive response.

A family vacation trip has been planned for months. Everyone is ready to depart from home in the morning, and then there is a phone call. A lifelong acquaintance that you have not seen for years has altered a business trip to stop by your house for a visit on the following afternoon. Or a distant family member who resides in another city is in trouble and needs to see you right away.

Every year you and your family celebrate this special day. However, this year on that very date the church has scheduled a special business meeting to discuss an important program of ministries. Your involvement at the meeting is needed for the entire evening.

You are writing hurriedly to complete a letter before the mailman arrives at your house. Unexpectedly, your next-door neighbor phones to indicate a pressing need to talk with you—not about matters of earthshaking importance but about trivia that are nonetheless important to those involved.

A deadline is staring you in the face and producing anxiety. Monthly reports are due. Right in the midst of frenzied paperwork, you look up and see a troubled fellow laborer standing in front of your desk. This longtime business associate has a problem at home and desperately wants your counsel right away.

You have been the organization's program chairperson for one year. Hours of preparation have piled up in advance of this unique audience-involvement event. Now, guests arrive who were not expected. These individuals do not want to participate in the activities of the evening, only to watch (cynically!). Why did visitors have to show up at this particular meeting?

You have waited until Saturday night to prepare for your Sunday responsibilities in church. Just as you begin to collect your thoughts, the doorbell rings. You greet a group of representatives from one of the leading community-help agencies. They want to discuss the possibilities of your personal involvement in their annual fund-raising campaign.

Finally you are on the plane. All day you have waited for this moment. You intend to read for a while and then sleep until you land at home. Suddenly your plans are shattered. The person seated next to you leans over and asks in a shaky voice, "Do you mind if I share a problem with you?"

We all know well the experience of inconveniences!

That life falls into such discontinuous or incongruent patterns is significant. In fact, the interspersion of problematic situations which call forth inconveniences helps make life what it is. In his book, *No Easy Victories*, John Gardner observed: "Total absence of problems would be the beginning of death for a society or an individual. We aren't constructed to live in that kind of world. We are problem-solvers by nature—problem-seekers, problem-requirers."[1]

Actually, individuals grow in their capabilities when their capabilities are challenged and stretched. An ability to make decisions, to develop sound emotional and behavioral reflexes, is dependent upon the nature of one's reactions to the sudden unexpected events which storm into life.

Though still difficult to accept, such inconveniences may be a blessing to the person of faith. This assessment is based upon the idea that a blessing is a visitation from God which creates an opportunity for encountering God. To claim a blessing is to be sensitive to God's presence in any given situation. Inconveniences may provide the most pregnant opportunities in life for persons to experience God and thus grow in faith.

Look at the matter biblically. Moses had enough trouble already. Pharaoh was after him because he had killed an Egyptian. His young marriage had recently produced a child. Trying to be responsible in the care of his father-in-law's flock of sheep, Moses came upon a bush burning with fire yet unconsumed. As if he did not previously have enough on his mind, Moses was confronted by God's call to become the leader of his people (Ex. 3:7–12).

Why is Moses remembered? Moses responded obediently to the call of God which came at an inconvenient moment amidst diverse and demanding responsibilities. Moses' maturation as a man of God occurred within a matrix of inconveniences. Interruptions in the life of this Hebrew leader were blessings which nurtured a greater faith and thus made life more meaningful.

Other intrusions with the potential for spiritual significance are recorded in the Bible. Do you remember the

Lord's visit to the household of Mary and Martha? Mary adjusted her schedule to benefit fully from the presence of Christ while Martha busied herself with domestic responsibilities and almost missed an opportunity of the ages (Luke 10:38–42). Recall how the pungent conversation between Cleopas and his fellow traveler was interrupted by a stranger. At first the two men seemed somewhat perturbed. While their hearts were heavy from reflections on the crucifixion of Jesus, this one who had joined them along the road exhibited no knowledge of the past week's turmoil. However, the stranger was drawn into dialogue and later was recognized as the risen Lord (Luke 24:13–31). The author of Hebrews demonstrated sensitivity to the spiritual promise of inconveniences when he warned his readers: "Do not neglect to show hospitality to strangers, for thereby some have entertained angels unawares" (13:2).

Do not be mistaken. Inconveniences do not confront people wearing a sign which reads "I am a blessing" or "I am an opportunity to grow in Christ." No! Inconveniences arise in individuals' lives looking just like what they are—troubles, problems, inconveniences.

Usually, people recognize inconveniences as blessings only in retrospect. Bothersome situations most frequently become significant for the persons involved only as they look back on the events. Historians and biographers may leave the wrong impression. By means of their writing skills they can neatly incorporate significant inconveniences into the story of a person or a nation so that the incidents do not appear to have been inconveniences at all. However, this is after the fact; a retrospective view.

Situations fraught with the potential for offering a blessing almost never come with clarity and dramatic preparation. Here is a man walking the streets begging for a meal when you are rushing to catch a cab—who would ever think this destitute individual presented an opportunity for serving Christ? Here is a family in need of clothing and someone to provide transportation to the doctor, but you barely have time to get home, change clothes, and be ready for a dinner engagement—who would ever believe that helping these ill-feeling and raggedly-clad people had anything to do with the kingdom of God? Those whom the church recognizes as true servants of Christ are believers who have laid hold of these kinds of inconveniences and either in the process or later have been surprised at how they were blessed by them.

True Christianity maintains a stance of openness so that God may be served wherever he is met. Generally, the new and exciting happens squarely in the midst of common ordinary moments. Dramatic encounters with the presence and power of God come within the hours of humdrum days. No trumpets announce such experiences. No parades precede them. No banners call attention to them. Yet, they come. Some people respond to inconveniences and experience the presence of God while others merely write off such situations as too bothersome to consider.

The basic principle involved—that inconveniences may be blessings—can be illustrated by numerous means. Two references, however, make the point. Both reflect recurring themes. Disruption may be more important in relation to God than that which they disrupt. Those events which seem to interfere with an individual's plans may be so significant as to dwarf the difficulties involved in a positive response to them.

Consider time. Inconveniences related to time may be a blessing in the sense that they remind persons of what time is for and to whom it ultimately belongs.

Periodically, individuals act as if they have forgotten what time is all about. A subtle kind of egocentrism tempts people to behave as if all of the universe must operate on their schedules. Thus, naturally, the church, the family, and all who need their assistance are expected to comply with their travel itineraries, appointments, and free time.

Certain events have a way of severely jogging presumptuous thoughts about time. Few people, if any, would have scheduled the birth of Christ halfway through a long journey or in the presence of stenching animals. For that matter, probably no one would have interrupted the beauty of the traditional Passover celebration with all of the virulent controversy over Jesus. Certainly, religiously-oriented individuals would not have spoiled the holiest season of the year with a crucifixion.

Obviously, God works on the basis of a clock [2] radically different in nature from the kind possessed by most folks. Sometimes his clock strikes at inconvenient hours. Those involved may have other priorities in mind but their plans are altered. God's time demands people's undivided attention.

Many passages in the Bible reflect an awareness of God's clock and an appreciation for its importance. Words from James are illustrative: "Come now, you who say, 'Today or tomorrow we will go into such and such a town and spend a year there and trade and get gain; whereas you do not know about tomorrow' " (4:13).

The best made plans of life are frequently interrupted by a different time—God's time—which comes crashing into the human experience. All activities are brought to a halt when death invades a home. A busy couple stops short of meeting all of their appointments when the time arrives for the birth of a child. In situations such as these, mechanical timepieces are of little importance and datebooks are irrelevant. Persons give themselves to the demands of the hour whether or not they are ready for the experience, despite other plans, and regardless of the inconveniences involved.

Who can understand divine chronology? A man is doing a good work in a key job and God calls him elsewhere to minister—why? A family has finally made the necessary adaptations and settled into an experimental mission endeavor with long-range significance when God leads them to a new place—why now, Lord? A woman has finally completed tedious preparation and embarked on her lifelong plans for a career when God summons her to a different work that will require more education and the development of new expertise—why such a sequence?

Paul was able to verbalize the emotional dilemma in which he found himself because of the ambiguity of time. Writing about the resurrection of Christ, he stated, "Last of all, as to one untimely born, he appeared also to me. For I am the least of the apostles unfit to be called an apostle, because I persecuted the church of God" (1 Cor. 15:8–9). Though the idea of inconvenience is not dominant in this passage, there is a clear indication of the awe with which this great missionary viewed God's time as it intersected his. Looking back, Paul saw the tremendous life-changing significance of that dramatic interruption which took place on the road to Damascus and altered all of his plans for the future.

Periodically, all people, without exception, need to be reminded that their present expenditures of time, the routines into which all of their efforts are harnessed, may not be the best. Inconveniences often bless persons by establishing that truth. Interruptions challenge hard and fast patterns of activity and raise questions regarding the manner in which God wants time to be used. After all, it is his time.

Consider also what inconveniences do to interpersonal relationships. How easy it is to become so engrossed in a job that the people involved are forgotten—fellow laborers, employers, employees, salespersons, consumers, friends, family members. Frantic efforts to complete those tasks which are deemed most important sometimes create blind spots to persons. People preoccupied with jobs are reminded of the primacy of persons only as some individual dares to assume the role of an intruder, an inconvenience. ("Daddy, when will you ever be able to stay home for an important meeting with the family?" "Son, do you not have any time in which you could get in even a brief visit with your mother and me?" "I thought we were friends but your allotments of time convey a different message!")

In one of Jesus' most familiar parables a man sitting on the side of the road needing help was bypassed by two men quite possibly on their way to or from the Temple. Perhaps their problem is similar to the perilous tendency among contemporary Christians—it is so imperative to get to the meeting, to give a part on the program, to complete an assignment, that there is no time for stopping, even to help a poor individual in trouble. Thus, the program or the meeting (the thing) receives adequate attention, the individual (the person) is ignored, and the potential blessing of an inconvenience is never realized. However, the person in Jesus' story who is best remembered as a prototype of God's kind of people is the man who let the needs of an abused individual take precedence over the requirements of his schedule. This sensitive servant experienced as well as demonstrated the grace of God.

Similar was the behavior of Jesus while on his way to the most important showdown in all of history. His mind was on Jerusalem and the conflict which awaited him there. His face was set toward that Holy City. Yet, at no point along the way did Jesus overlook those who lined the roads asking for help. Even on the journey to the cross there was time to interrupt his steps of destiny so that the blind, the crippled, and the sick could be healed.

Persons must be forever more important than things—than assignments, than jobs, than schedules, than meetings. The truth of this statement may be best validated by a compassionate response to personal needs which requires some inconvenience but which promises an experience with God.

These thoughts do not constitute a plea for chaotic living. No suggestion is made that all planned schedules be junked and that every act be done spontaneously. The central concern is that persons never become so locked into any one pattern of life that provisions cannot be made for dealing with intrusions, especially, inconvenient ones. It just may be that the interruption is more important than the routine, that the inconvenient is of far more significance than the convenient.

Inconvenient moments often constitute a blessing. A positive response to inconvenient demands may usher one into the presence of God and evoke more faithful service to Christ. Hopefully the day will come when prayerful thanksgivings can be offered to God for the inconveniences of life as well as for the conveniences.

The Danger Of The Commonplace

"You must not call what God has cleansed common."
Acts 10:15 (Phillips)

"And God, who studies each commonplace soul,
Out of commonplace things makes His beautiful whole."
SARAH CHAUNCEY WOOLSEY

4
The Danger Of The Commonplace

"Anything is possible" appears to be the blasé philosophy of contemporary culture. Citizens in today's world have traveled farther and seen more, either personally by means of rapid transit systems or vicariously by means of the media, than members of any previous generation. An individual's ability to be shocked is almost a thing of the past.

Surprise is an emotion now generally relegated to children and associated with weakness. Wonder is disguised, if experienced at all, while imperturbability is flaunted. Suave shoulder-shrugging accompanied by a passive "so what?" has replaced startled looks and spontaneous uninhibited exclamations in the face of impressive inventions and novel revelations. Even the most highly unusual phenomena fail to gain sustained attention since they are considered but the first expressions of matters which will become habitual. Such a bland mentality is the recent product of a segment of history in which . . .

Change has reverberated throughout society like a sonic boom rattling every structure, threatening ecological balance, and attracting the attention of even the most detached individuals.

Dread diseases of the past have been made almost extinct by spectacular laboratory findings passed on to the public by way of new medications for illnesses and innovative methods of preventive health care. Major organ transplants have promised an increased longevity to lives in which the "last days" were previously numbered.

A tidal wave of violent crime has swept across the nation's legal dikes flooding cities, spilling over into rural villages, and leaving in its wake freaked-out drug addicts, discredited public officials, overextended law enforcement officers, assassinated political leaders, and a manic public. Hospitable America characterized by open doors and welcome mats for all was turbulently transformed into a frightened America with multilocked doors and neurotic citizens suspicious even of their closest neighbors.

Under the shadow of a mushroom-shaped cloud, youngsters were enlisted in military involvements to save democracy and to end all future wars. High hopes for peace, however, were badly shaken by the Korean conflict and almost totally shattered in the jungles and rice paddies of Southeast Asia.

Patriots in "the land of the free" have realized that "liberty and justice for all" are noble ideals which have never become realities for major segments of the population. Even those who resent various groups demanding "freedom now!" find themselves uncomfortable with increased infringements on personal liberties in their own homes.

Witnesses to the advent of automotive transportation on earth have observed, by means of television, extravehicular excursions on the surface of the moon. The traditional aesthetic pleasure derived from gazing at that dominant nighttime luminary has been enhanced by the staggering realization that men have traveled in outer space, landed on the lunar sphere, and returned to this earth with cosmic souvenirs.

. . . People no longer speak with cynicism regarding possibilities for the future. Mechanical inventions and social innovations have been so numerous as to be considered monotonous. Reformations have almost overrun each other. Major crises and their solutions have occurred with hypnotic frequency. Fantasies have become realities. The spectacular is now expected as merely another aspect of the ordinary.

Contemporary human beings are not easily moved by anything. Everything has been ushered into the realm of the possible. No one matter seems any more important than any other matter. All things are accepted calmly, even passively. Some social observers label this phenomenon as progress. Surely progress is involved. However, the dominant spirit of the times does not reflect progress. When all of life is categorized as commonplace, apathy is the accompanying emotion and deterioration the likely prospect.

Christianity has not been immune to the spreading infection of society's nonchalant spirit. In a situation where people are bombarded from every side with luring advertisements, news flashes, historical documentaries, and gracious invitations; crucial statements and sublime actions of the Judeo-Christian faith have been cast among the commonalities of life. Hence a cultural climate now exists which threatens the church even more than hostile opposition. When Christianity is relegated to a commonplace status in life, when it is forced into a position alongside everything else, it is poised to die. The Christian church has always fared better when threatened and bitterly persecuted than when taken for granted and nominally supported.

When considered common, Christianity is robbed of its uniqueness and the "idea of the holy" is smothered under the tranquilizing press of the ordinary. Profound scriptural truths like "God is love" (1 John 4:8) are lost among promotional declarations like "Coke is the real thing." Admonishments such as "the kingdom of God is at hand; repent, and believe in the gospel" (Mark 1:15), which evoke a response of eternal consequences, are heard and heeded with no more intensity than that devoted to Park Avenue sales instructions such as, "Brush your teeth with Colgate." Danger abounds.

Back in the early 1900s those who listened to the lectures or read the books of John Henry Jowett were warned against becoming overly familiar with either the sublime or the commonplace. In the first instance, according to this great preacher, one may be "fussily busy about the Holy Place" but "lose the wondering sense of the Holy Lord."[1] Similarly, in the case of the second concern, Jowett observed that "A stupor begotten of familiarity" may cause one to be "remote from the common need."[2]

Disastrous is that attitude which reduces the sublime to the ordinary and views the major recurring events of life as common. Under the influence of such a mentality, individuals make no major decisions because nothing is viewed as major. Morality becomes optional, other people appear expendable, and religion seems out of place.

Most individuals have learned firsthand that a longtime familiarity with matters tends to breed a judgment that these matters are common. For this very reason, some of the greatest obstacles to an in-depth faith, characteristic of mature Christianity, exist within the church. Having grown up in the heritage of the church, if not within its very confines, many believers allow their familiarity with the institution to blind them to its continuing authority as the divinely-willed household of faith. The essential message of the church has been proclaimed with such regularity that numerous persons now take pulpit communication for granted and consider the demands of preaching with a "take it or leave it" mind-set appropriate for Saturday morning cartoons. Even though organized religion is made a part of life's routine by millions of people, faith is forced to stand alongside the school, civic organizations, economics, politics, recreational activities, and other personal involvements. In summary, church is considered *just* another place to go and Christianity *merely* the source of additional responsibilities.

The cataract of deadening familiarity which hampers Christian vision and impedes progression in the Christian pilgrimage must be removed. Persons caught in the crippling grip of the mundane must be set free. Only then can the uniqueness of Christianity produce the kind of authentic excitement which precipitates a spiritual quest that ends in redemption and sustains a journey of faith that leads to maturity. Three affirmations point the way.

Christianity knows no common church.

"Common" and "ordinary" are adjectives grammatically acceptable but theologically untenable when used to modify the noun "church." The very nature of the noun mitigates against the correctness of the adjectives. The Christian church is not *just* another institution in society.

Popularity has proven troublesome for the church. Contemporary Christians meeting regularly in stained-glass architecture are far removed from those days in the Roman Empire when the Christian faith was considered illegal and when worshipers were forced to convene in the catacombs. The Christian church is now categorized as one of the major "charitable," "patriotic," and "worthy" institutions in society. Movement toward this new level of recognition and acceptance has been somewhat detrimental to the church. Today individuals relate to the church with a commitment similar to that allotted to the local lodge, a civic club, or some professional organization. The words of the church receive little more thoughtful consideration than that devoted to the text of an evening newscast.

Rightly understood, the church is never common. That fact merits recognition, affirmation, and action on the part of every Christian. Support for the church should transcend any other institutional loyalty. Attentiveness to the church's message must be qualitatively more profound than that devoted to the barrage of messages beamed by secular media. The church cannot be *like* everything else or, for that matter, anything else. The church is not so much an institution of society as a community of destiny.

That company of people called by God to be his servants in the world makes up the church. In biblical terminology these constitute the "body of Christ" (Eph. 4:13). The church is the extension of Christ into every generation. Its ministry is patterned after Christ's ministry. Its message is the message which Jesus came preaching. Thus, within the church exists an individual's only hope for redemption, for learning how to live with God, the best hope for fellowship, and learning how to live with other persons.

Care must be taken lest an honest desire for regular involvement in the corporate rites of worship be reduced to a pseudo-commitment which finds expression in entrenched routines. Individual believers ought to guard against the tendency of transforming the conscientious practice of church-related disciplines into mindless participation of holy habits. Familiarity with the church simply must not breed apathy.

Where the church gathers, people should join in the kind of praise which glorifies God and strengthens personal faith. When the church meets, sinners should confess their sins in an environment of forgiveness. As the church prays, persons plagued by troubles should share their heavy loads and find rest for their weary souls. While the church speaks, individuals should learn of a redemption which gives meaning to life in this world and security for the life to come. In the church's ministries, care should be given to the physical and spiritual needs of both individuals and society.

Christianity knows no common church!

Christianity recognizes no common person.

First-century Jews had trouble relating to anyone other than individuals out of their own tradition. Even the basic Old Testament commandment regarding love for neighbor was reduced to a narrow mandate applicable only to Jewish neighbors. Jesus' ministry challenged head-on and sought to eradicate completely such a biased view of interpersonal relations.

Prejudice was the problem with which Peter was wrestling in the tenth chapter of Acts. Association with Gentiles had brought down upon him the anger of racially prejudiced Jews. No doubt, Peter was being chided as a "Gentile lover." An honest openness toward all people produced by his Christian experience was in mortal conflict with the restricted realm of relational involvements prescribed by his background and by some of his peers. Finally, after painful revisions in his social relationships, Peter confessed, "God has shown me that I should not call any man common or unclean" (Acts 10:28). What an insight!

Christianity asserts that every person is created in the image of God and affirms every individual as a being of infinite worth. Absolutely no one stands outside the multitude of people upon whom Christ looked with compassion and for whom he died. Thus, followers of Christ must ask in every instance, "Who am I to look at anyone created in God's image, anyone for whom Christ died, and judge that person to be common?"

Sensitive Christians take seriously the life and situation of every person met. Both big and little events alike are considered consequential. Though births and deaths occur with the staccato regularity of seconds ticking off of a tightly-wound clock, they can never be accepted as ordinary. When life comes into this world, rejoicing is to be shared. When a life departs from this world, grief is to be shared. Real Christians never forget either how to laugh or how to cry. The lives of people and the events which fill those lives are so far beyond the status of common that they merit unhindered attention.

History bears witness to numerous tragic situations in which people have been viewed as common and thus treated as expendable. The two go hand in hand. Anytime one individual judges another individual as common or unimportant, the judgmental person may use, abuse, and even destroy the judged one. Does it not happen every day?

Among the Nazis in Germany, Jews were labeled "expendable" and lined up for extermination. In Communist Russia, the Kulaks were cruelly eliminated from Soviet society because they were considered common people and in the way of the revolution. How is it where we live? Who do we consider to be common people, the expendable individuals, where we live—the poor, the blacks, the uneducated, the elderly, the Indians, the hungry? When Christians can spend exorbitantly, dress lavishly, eat gorgingly, and sleep soundly while people are underfed, ill clothed, sick, and mistreated; Christians have become too common.

Christianity recognizes no common person!

Christianity produces no common faith.

Jesus' call to discipleship is more than just another mundane consideration that an individual may or may not choose thoughtfully to entertain. "If any man would come after me, let him deny himself and take up his cross and follow me" (Matt. 16:24), is an invitation—a confrontation—which demands a decision that affects one's total destiny.

Unfortunately, familiarity with Jesus' summons to a new quality of life has deadened some people's sensitivity to the critical implications of their response. Likewise, faith for many people is an ambiguous phenomenon which they expect ministers to talk about, churches to promote, and children to accept. These are the individuals who secretly conclude that real faith is a good thought to ponder but an impractical way of life to assume. For such persons, religious faith is just another matter which demands attention. As decisions are made about daily menus, monthly budgets, and annual vacations, some thought is devoted to the need for faith.

The cruciality of Christian faith can be neglected only with serious consequences. Christian faith is not just another doctrine, philosophy, noble idea, or way of life set among other doctrines, philosophies, ideas, and life-styles. Rather, it is the one way in which life can be lived with complete meaning and purpose. Only through faith in Christ can a person be reconciled to God. Only in Christian faith can people find all of the resources which enable them to live together in peace. Christian faith pervades all of life establishing a redemptive balance between repentance and forgiveness, memory and hope, contemplation and activism, good news and judgment, private and corporate worship, and belief and behavior.

Christianity produces no common faith!

In C. S. Lewis' classic *The Screwtape Letters,* a senior devil writes to a junior devil explaining how people may be lured away from God and confined to the domain of evil. The older devil observes that the people he is trying to influence are enslaved by the pressures of the ordinary. Advising the junior devil on how to "convert" a client, he says, "Keep pressing home on him the *ordinariness* of things."[3]

Though not always audibly heard, the word is out that life is common. Koheleth is not dead (Eccl. 1:1–2). There are still those people who propagate the impression that nothing is new, nothing is important, nothing is unique, nothing merits excitement, and nothing deserves a commitment of life. Do not believe it!

Think through the matter. Almighty God has become incarnate in Jesus Christ and called upon all people to join him in a redemptive fellowship. This great God has pointed the way toward peaceful relationships and demonstrated how that way may be traveled. His Son, the Savior of the world, has bequeathed to all generations a church equipped to carry on the word and work of salvation. To all who will trust in him, God has given a faith founded on truth, encouraged by hope, and expressed in love. What is described here is not like anything else. A very uncommon God has acted in unusual ways and now calls upon all people to live with him in a manner that is extraordinary.

Christians will do well to pray daily that never by either word or deed will anything which is the work of God be relegated to the status of common.

The Privilege Of Temptation

"No temptation has come your way that is too hard for flesh and blood to bear. But God can be trusted not to allow you to suffer any temptation beyond your powers of endurance. He will see to it that every temptation has a way out, so that it will never be impossible for you to bear it."

1 Corinthians 10:13 (Phillips)

"Why comes temptation, but for man to meet
And master and make crouch beneath his foot,
And so be pedestaled in triumph?"

ROBERT BROWNING

5
The Privilege Of Temptation

Apparently temptations are a part of the stuff of which life in this world is made. No one is immune to temptations. If we do not go to the wilderness, the wilderness comes to us.

Temptation wears many masks. Critical moments of moral decision making arise in numerous situations . . .

> A young success-oriented businessman discovers an illegal but well-hidden income tax adjustment that he can make. Chances of any punishment are small. The amount of badly-needed money which could be gained is substantial.
>
> During the monthly meeting of her social club, a young woman is suddenly faced with an opportunity to express a damaging opinion of another member. Strong dislike for this individual repressed in silence for many years could now be verbalized with a satisfying sense of retribution.
>
> An unbelievably heavy schedule of activities confronts the family over a period of several months. With ease, regular attendance in church can be shifted from the status of a top priority involvement to that of a desirable goal delayed for future attention.
>
> Two young people discover in each other the kind of relationship which nurtures a joyous love. Their outings together make any kind of restraint on emotions and

discipline in actions seem totally inappropriate.

A knowledgeable financial consultant meets with an uninformed but trusting client. Without any questions being asked, a small-print clause, profitable to the consultant but costly to the client, can be written into a contractual agreement.

Problems confronting the organization are complex. The president of the company, whose term of office will end in just two months, sees an answer. A simple solution can be proposed. However, the simplicity of the solution is sure to create even greater difficulties for the next president.

Demands imposed by "things"—meetings to be attended, projects to be concluded, repairs to be made, trips to be taken, bills to be paid—become almost intolerable. Pressures related to possessions, achievement, and status, border on being unbearable. While frantically attempting to get away from such demands and out from under such pressures, people—spouses, children, friends—begin to appear more like objects in the way than persons to be loved.

. . . Lists of temptations vary from individual to individual. But every person has a private inventory.

Temptation is so integral to the makeup of human existence that the greatest commentary on life ever written, the Bible, has been called the "Book of Temptations."[1] From Genesis (3:1–7), in which the first man and the first woman succumb to temptation, to Revelation (3:10), in which readers are warned of the "hour of trial which is coming on the whole world," temptation is a constant scriptural theme. Spanning the space between biblical accounts of the creation and the culmination of life in this world is a history of the people of God and histories of godly people. Both embrace a continuous chain of temptations which stretches even into the present. Temptations stalked Abraham, challenged Jesus, and trouble contemporaries.

Certain persistent questions are provoked by the fact of temptation: How are we to contend with temptation? Are we to despair of it and run from it? Should we attempt a monastic existence, retreating behind walls erected to withstand the lure of the world? Or, could it be that we must face temptation like we face other facts of life and seek to deal with it as a way to strength rather than weakness. Dare we go so far as to see temptation as a privilege?

Satisfactory answers to these important questions require an accurate understanding of what temptation means. The biblical term usually translated as "temptation" carries a meaning far more comprehensive than the contemporary concept of temptation. A clarity in understanding is important.

New Testament writers employed the same word to denote both trials and temptations. (Exemplary is the discussion in Jas. 1:12–13.) In some instances temptation referred to testing (Jas. 1:12). Just as swords, reputations, and prophets could be tested, so could faith. A crisis in one's family, economic loss, illness, and political persecution were tempters. In other instances temptation referred to an enticement to evil (Jas. 1:13). Where this latter meaning was dominant, the issue was not a test of faith but an invitation to abandon faith. The dilemma of the person tempted involved the attractiveness of evil rather than the severity of testing.

God is not the author of either phenomenon. Inevitably someone raises the question, "Does God cause temptations?" The answer of the Bible is "no." James stated this truth unequivocally: "Let no one say when he is tempted, 'I am tempted by God'; for God cannot be tempted with evil and he himself tempts no one" (Jas. 1:13). To *permit* temptations to occur and to *cause* temptations to occur are two very different matters. In granting freedom for his creation, God allows for the possibility of temptations. However, God never seeks to draw people into experiences which could ultimately separate them from his redemptive love.

Personal experience corroborates the New Testament understanding of temptation. Trials and enticements to evil do plague people's lives. Yet, paradoxically, temptation may be a way to God as well as a challenge to God's way. Historically those people most recognizable as persons of faith have been individuals to whom trials and temptations were not strangers.

While the harassment of temptation is a negative force, opportunities made possible by temptation are pregnant with positive potential. William Barclay wrote of the tests which beset a Christian's life and recorded this judgment regarding them: "But the whole point of them is that they are not sent to make us fall; they are sent to make us soar. They are not sent to defeat us; they are sent that we may defeat them. They are not sent to make us weaker; they are sent to make us stronger."[2] In the midst of temptation, recreative forces are set into motion. Temptation can be a privilege.

Temptation frequently facilitates much needed self-understanding.

The author of Hebrews correctly emphasized the importance of Jesus' experience—"one who in every respect has been tempted as we are" (4:15)—as a model for understanding the privilege of temptation. From the first hours to the final days of his public ministry, Jesus dealt with temptation so as to know himself better and to envision his task more clearly.

Having decided to embark upon his public ministry from the baptismal waters of the Jordan River, Jesus immediately had to withstand the protests of John the Baptist—"I need to be baptized by you" (Matt. 3:14)—in order to identify himself with the people whom he would save. Then came the extended desert dialogue with Satan. Jesus' concept of himself as Messiah and of his ministry as messianic was severely tested by the taunts of evil. His ultimate commitment to the way of the Suffering Servant was forged in the heat and tested by the flames of temptations which pointed to the viability of an economic, military, or magical messiahship.

Though Jesus' testing in the wilderness was completed after forty days, he was not finished with temptation. Time after time in his ministry seductive situations arose which provoked clarifications of who he was and what he was about.

When Jesus came to Gethsemane during those final stormy days in Jerusalem, the temptations of the wilderness became the temptations of the garden. Once again the Lord wrestled with evil, with himself, and with God. Had it not been for the understanding which Jesus gained during that tumultuous night of trial, one wonders if he would have had the strength to face a cross. However, the strength was his. In the midst of burdensome temptations he had discovered God's confirmation of his servant ministry.

Because Jesus had been to the wilderness and to the garden, because he had found himself as well as God in those continuous hours of trial which stood like minute markers on the timepiece of his ministry, he could go to the cross. Questions of tempting alternatives had been resolved. Only convictions remained—he was the Suffering Servant, he was the Messiah who had to die, and he was the king whose throne was to be a cross.

Most individuals both discover and reveal who they are in face-to-face combat with temptation. When existence is stretched to the extremities—during the most trying times of the week when fatigue is maximal and resistance is minimal; when the boredom imposed by lengthy stretches of commonplace days tempts one to break the routine at any expense—a person's true identity emerges. The insights into personhood evidenced in these situations are tremendously important. Apart from facade, pretenses, and hypocrisy, here is the real self. Known now at least to the person involved and perhaps even to acquaintances is the nature of this individual's strengths, needs, sins, faith, and hope. From such understanding help can come.

The significant effect of temptation upon a person's nature is most obvious during periods of moral decision making. When an individual grapples with choices between right and wrong much more is at stake than the immediate outcome of the dilemma. A struggle is underway with evil, the self, and God. About to be exposed is the essence of personhood—here is an individual with strong moral convictions and a courageous commitment to remain faithful to them; or here is an individual whose moral strength is proportionate to the ease of the actions required; here is a person of genuine faith or here is a person in need of faith. Decisions made in seemingly isolated events with apparently minor consequences become the foundations upon which major decisions with wide-ranging implications are made.

All people need to know who they are. Only then can the reality of weaknesses, doubts, and passivity be replaced by strengths, convictions, and constructive action. Only then can negative qualities be eliminated and positive qualities reinforced. Temptation frequently facilitates much needed self-understanding.

Temptation may also encourage spiritual maturity.

Persons who attempt to avoid all of the unpleasant, immoral, and ugly aspects of life retard their spiritual development. Maturation in faith does not take place in a vacuum. The world with all of its trials and temptations to evil is the very environment in which Christian discipleship is to be accepted, nurtured, and lived.

The principle of growth in stress is recognized in other dimensions of life as well as in the spiritual. Athletes prepare for competitive events by subjecting themselves to unusual stress—boxers prepare for championship bouts by sparring with extra-heavy gloves just as sprinters ready themselves for a big race by wearing weighted shoes while they run. Employers want to know the past work records of potential employees in order to discover how their basic skills have fared when tested by the demanding pressures of daily difficulties.

Strength in Christian character—growth in faith, wisdom, grace, hope, and love—emerges from participation in periods of testing and confrontations with immorality. Trials tend to put people in touch with those matters which are of ultimate importance; to take people to the depths in which renewal may be begun. The apostle Paul gave voice to this truth in his confession to the Romans: "We rejoice in our sufferings, knowing that suffering produces endurance, and endurance produces character, and character produces hope, and hope does not disappoint us because God's love has been poured into our hearts through the Holy Spirit which has been given to us" (5:3–5).

Abraham was a man of faith. From the moment he ventured out of Ur of the Chaldees until the end of his life, a vital trust in God dominated his pilgrimage. Yet, for Abraham just as for other spiritual giants whose lives are recounted in the Scriptures, an already strong faith became even stronger as a result of numerous crises. Exemplary was Abraham's traumatic decision to offer his son Isaac as a sacrifice to God.

Having traveled among pagans and witnessed their morbid ritual of child sacrifice to a false god, Abraham may have wondered about the strength of his faith in the true God. Testing questions could have troubled his conscience and tempestuous doubts challenged his convictions: "Is my faith sufficient for that kind of demand? Do I love the true God as much as those pagans seem to love their false god? Would I give up my own son in order to serve God?"

Self-imposed testing took Abraham to the precipice of tragedy. However, this was a place of revelation and a time of growth. Abraham departed from the mountain in the land of Moriah with Isaac his son, a better understanding of the nature of his God, and a more mature faith. Individuals whose faith has never been questioned by doubts, tried by crises, challenged by evil, and tested by difficulties are very likely people who do not really know the depths of their faith. Paradoxically, the very experiences which tempt persons to stumble, fall, or even fail completely are occasions in which persons discover whether or not they can in fact walk with God and be assured that his presence is all they need. Frequently the greatest challenges to spiritual development offer the most potent incentives to spiritual development, to grow up in Christ.

Temptation may be the occasion for a vision of God and the motivation to seek fellowship among the people of God.

Recognition of the need for resources outside the self and a desire for spiritual fellowship with like-minded individuals are often born out of a person's struggle to endure the pain of testing and to withstand the lure of temptation. Operative are phenomena similar to those so clearly discernible in the respectable, vital, and successful organization known as Alcoholics Anonymous. Persons with a common problem admit their need for help and seek a solution to their difficulty in supportive relationships. Great is the potential in such a situation for an encounter with God and enlistment with God's kind of people.

Unfortunately some persons fail to recognize their need for God until a situation of desperation arises. Strangely enough the chaotic disorientation precipitated by temptation often serves as the prelude to a proper perspective on life. Priorities are reordered as the fundamentals of life become unmistakably clear: succumb to temptation and prepare for its certain consequences—"the wages of sin is death" (Rom. 6:23—or follow Christ and grow in the fulfillment of his promise—"do this and you will live" (Luke 10:28). God's redemptive nature is understood as never before.

Persons who are just about utterly to be defeated by evil are usually more eager to seek God than to theorize regarding the possibility of his existence, to pray than to debate the efficacy of prayer, to learn from the Scriptures than to scoff concerning their relevance, and to unite with sinners who have been saved by grace than to castigate the saved as hypocritical sinners. Apathy regarding spiritual salvation and passivity concerning communication with God tend to disappear amidst a frantic search for some way out of life-consuming personal problems and an earnest desire for helpful counsel. The admonition of Christ is finally heeded: "Watch and pray that you may not enter into temptation" (Matt. 26:41).

The church confesses as its Lord one who knew the difficulty of encounters with temptation (The author of Hebrews said of Christ, "He himself has suffered and been tempted"—2:18.), and embraces in its membership persons who face temptations daily, and claims as its promise a faith sufficient to overcome temptations. Thus, individuals engaged in a life-and-death bout with evil may well turn to the church for the help needed to mature in their understanding of God, to be faithful in their followship of Christ, and to be honest with their own best selves. Within the fellowship of God's people are the hope of defeating temptation, resources to aid in the realization of that hope, forgiveness for those who have failed, and affirmation for those who have succeeded. The church is a community of the tempted who ultimately will not be defeated.

The way to overcome temptation is synonymous with the path which leads to a relationship with God and fellowship with God's people. When on the verge of spiritually dying alone, one discovers the value of life in relationships. When on the edge of defeat by evil, one moves to the threshold of that victory inherent in righteousness. When in the face of a cynical and decadent depression one senses the spiritual promise which instills hope, something good happens. No wonder Martin Luther could posit that only an enemy of Christ would desire that life be free from all trials.

When a life is turned toward Christ by a moment of severe trial or temptation, the nature of that moment itself is not changed. Trial remains trouble. Evil remains evil. However, what happened in that moment to alter the nature of the future in such a positive manner is so great a blessing that the moment itself seems to have been a privilege.

Please do not misunderstand. The point of this essay is that the results of temptation can be positive in nature; temptation can be a privilege. In no way is this to suggest that persons should seek out temptations or invite periods of testing. Individuals should no more search for temptations in order to grow than they should look down a poisonous snake's throat for information. What has been written above is a recognition of the reality of temptation and its potential, not a commendation of temptation.

Here is no suggestion that temptation is intriguing, easy, or the source of fun. To be caught up in an experience of temptation is to feel one's self in the throes of hell. However, here is the observation that the security which accompanies a redemptive relationship with God may be more readily recognizable when one has experienced the insecurity of tumultuous temptations, that the beauty of life in Jesus Christ is more easily discernible when one has witnessed the ugliness of evil. Never is the sun so bright as when one steps from the fears and frustrations of total darkness into the clarifying brilliance of its light. So it is with movement from the turmoil of an enticing engagement with evil into the tranquillity of a saving experience with God.

Temptation is to be avoided if at all possible. Our prayer to God remains "lead us not into temptation" (Matt. 6:13). However, when temptation comes, we should be aware that it carries both a positive and a negative potential. Temptation may strengthen instead of weaken, inspire instead of disparage, and lead to God as well as away from God. We need not run from temptation.

The positive potential of temptation is assured by the divine promise of a means for coping with temptation. Paul verbalized the grand assurance: "God is faithful, and he will not let you be tempted beyond your strength, but with the temptation will also provide the way of escape, that you may be able to endure it" (1 Cor. 10:13). Temptation is a privilege because God's grace is sufficient for every situation!

Costly Grace

"For all alike have sinned, and are deprived of the divine splendour, and all are justified by God's free grace alone, through his act of liberation in the person of Christ Jesus."
Romans 3:23–24 (NEB)

*"Cheap grace is the deadly enemy of our Church.
We are fighting to-day for costly grace."*
DIETRICH BONHOEFFER

6
Costly Grace

Dominant in the language of the church from the first century to the present has been the word grace. Followers of Jesus Christ have praised the reality of grace, meditated upon the meaning of grace, and witnessed concerning the power of grace. Historically grace has been the focal point in greetings ("Grace to you.") and benedictions ("Grace be with you."), in confessions of faith ("God's grace is sufficient!"), in recitations of Scripture ("For by grace you have been saved through faith; and this is not your own doing, it is the gift of God." Eph. 2:8), in prayers of intercession ("May the grace of God bring peace."), and in songs of praise ("Amazing Grace"). Currently grace-talk is so prevalent that the word often is bandied about more lightly than its meaning permits.

The great German theologian and Christian martyr Dietrich Bonhoeffer made a splendid contribution to Christendom with his insights regarding the meaning of grace. In his disturbing work, *The Cost of Discipleship,* Bonhoeffer coined the phrases "cheap grace" and "costly grace" and carefully distinguished each from the other.[1] Bonhoeffer's profound thoughts inspired and informed the following reflection on the uncommon element of grace in the common life of a Christian.

Costly grace is the means of personal redemption.

Viewed either from the perspective of God's participation in personal redemption or from amidst the plight of persons being redeemed, the truth is the same. That grace which is operative in the redemptive act is costly beyond measure.

Consider grace from the divine perspective. Prominent in the early chapters of Genesis is God's intention to create persons, volitional creatures with dignity and worth, to whom he could relate with love. From the first moment in which the breath of life filled human nostrils, God expressed concern for the height of his creation and sought fellowship with living souls. However, the compassion of the Creator God was spurned by creaturely people bent more upon rebellion than relationships. These pilgrims on a virgin planet were too restless within themselves to recognize the divine sovereignty which could give meaning, purpose, and joy to their journey.

Humankind decided to make their own rules, chart their own course, and somehow provide for themselves whatever redemption they might need. The transcendent source of life was ignored. The fellowship which God had intended, initiated, and encouraged was violated. Finite individuals attempted to act like the infinite deity. As a result, the divine-human relationship was severed. Life was split into the "sacred" and the "secular." Those who desired to be the architects of their own destiny constructed by disobedience a cosmic partition constituted by sin. The beauty of a harmonious creation was marred by a gaudy barrier which now stood between those created in the image of God and God himself.

The Genesis account of disruption in the divine-human relationship is descriptive of a continuing phenomenon. What happened in the Garden of Eden occurred again at the foot of Mount Sinai, on the plains of Moab, by the river

Chebar, along the Jericho road, in the Valley of Jezreel, and at other sites all over the world. Something was wrong throughout creation.

An understandable assessment of this situation on the part of God could well have led to a declaration of terminal judgment: "I'm through with these people. I have saved them from numerous disasters of their own making, offered them forgiveness when punishment was more appropriate, and called them back into fellowship when I could have bidden them good-bye. Repeatedly they have been deaf to my efforts at communication and insensitive to my expressions of compassion. They seem preoccupied with going their own way even if destruction is the end of it. I give up." Justice alone would permit such a conclusion and provoke such action.

Though God is a just God, he is also a God of grace. The divine disposition toward a wayward creation was shaped more by grace than by justice. God seemed to reason: "I am separated from the people I love by a barrier which I did not make. For fellowship between us ever to be restored that obstacle must be obliterated. However, the initiative has to be mine. Human beings do not have the power within themselves to correct the wrong they have done, to remove the wall which they have erected."

God knew the price of a redemptive relationship with his people. Transcendence would have to give way to involvement in the human situation. Without a doubt, the redemptive pilgrimage of incarnation would ultimately be interrupted by a cross.

Some thoughtful bystander interested in salvation history and intoxicated with justice might well at this point blurt out an admonishment to God: "No! Don't do that! The people don't deserve it. You have no more obligations to them!" The bystander would be correct. However, grace, not justice, was the decisive factor in God's deliberation. He resolved to break the barrier even if this meant some brokenness for himself.

When God became incarnate on the earth he had created, few people took significant notice. Individuals continued their rebellion against the divine will. Most people neither prepared for Jesus' coming nor welcomed his presence. God's mission of salvation met head-on with a human passion for life without God. Those same sinister sentiments which sought to push God out of the Garden of Eden now sought to get him out of Jerusalem and even out of the world.

To describe what God did in Christ as grace is a statement of fact. To posit that this grace was costly is an understatement of reality. By means of suffering, pain, loneliness, and a cross, Christ broke the barrier erected by sin and restored the possibility of meaningful human repentance, divine forgiveness, and divine-human fellowship. Costly grace is the means of personal redemption from the perspective of God.

Consider grace from the human perspective. A confrontation with God's action in Jesus Christ requires a personal response. Every individual, either consciously or subconsciously, engages in a decision making process regarding the divine-human relationship.

Ultimate questions are provoked and radical commitments are elicited by a consideration of God's redemptive mission. A person is made to ponder: "Who am I?" and "What is *my* relationship to God?" Answers to these questions are evaluated in terms of both immediate and eternal consequences: "If I should seek to live apart from God—direct my activities, set my priorities, and deal with my problems alone—what are the likely results both in this life and the life to come?"

Such self-introspection may cause personal confessions regarding the dominance of sin, a lack of purpose and meaning, the inadequacy of human resources alone, and the need for help. This is the point at which some decision is made: "I will face life apart from any transcendent reference and take my chances in handling whatever may come my way as a result," or "I now confess my inadequacy to live apart from God, accept God's forgiveness, and affirm my trust in God as the sole source of authority in my life."

The costly nature of grace and its vital role in the redemptive process are best understood at the moment a decision is made to reach out for God's help. A desperately impatient desire for forgiveness which would wrest it from the heavens if possible must patiently wait for the gift of forgiveness which can come from God alone. A sincere longing for salvation which motivates a willingness to do anything necessary to earn it is tempered with the truth that salvation cannot be merited, bargained for, or forced.

Genuine gratitude for grace is born out of the interaction of one's readiness to rely upon God in the present and one's remembrance of how God has been treated in the past. "All of these years I have turned my back to God. Why should he accept me now? Justice says he will not do it." The reasoning goes on. However, before these thoughts can pass from the mind there comes the astounding word of God's forgiveness and the surge of joy inherent in redemption. God acts out of grace!

Mistakenly, some people assume that since salvation is a gift which must be received, it comes by means of a grace that is cheap and an acceptance that is easy. Such an errant judgment is possible only when the centrality of the cross has been overlooked and the nature of discipleship misunderstood.

Alan Walker has pointed out that there are two crosses of

extreme importance in the New Testament.[2] One is the cross of Christ. The second cross is that to which Jesus calls his disciples—"everybody's Calvary."[3] The first cross is essential in the experience of salvation and the second cross is essential in the life of the one who is saved. Crucified on the cross of identification are all of those dimensions of life—ambitions, calendars, relationships, agendas, prestige—which retard growth in grace and prohibit development in discipleship. Pain arises as the follower of Christ shoulders the "daily crosses" and chooses to do the right thing rather than the easy, expected, or expedient thing. When the cross is central, grace is costly.

Discipleship means following Jesus as well as believing in Jesus. Far more is involved than a profession of faith and identification with a local church. An unconditional commitment to Christ must be made and uncompromising obedience to Christ must ensue. Every dimension of life—work and words, rest and recreation, family and finances, prayer and politics, individual integrity and social responsibility—is affected. One's total being is subsumed under the lordship of Christ.

Jesus' consistent summons to discipleship spelled out the demands of his way: "If any man would come after me, let him deny himself and take up his cross and follow me" (Mark 8:34). Bonhoeffer correctly caught the extreme of Christ's invitation in his terse and shocking statement: "When Christ calls a man, he bids him come and die."[4] When the nature of discipleship is understood, grace is costly.

Illustrative of the human perspective on costly grace is Simon Peter's development in discipleship. In response to a question from Jesus regarding people's understanding of him, Peter gave voice to a profound insight: "You are the Christ, the Son of the living God" (Matt. 16:15). Commendation and praise for the disciple's statement were immediate. At this moment grace seemed cheap. However, when the conversation moved from a mere confession of discipleship to consideration of the ministry of the Messiah, the costly nature of grace emerged.

In response to Jesus' explanation "that he must go to Jerusalem and suffer," the bold affirmation from Peter so eloquently stated just moments earlier became a stern rebuke: "God forbid, Lord! This shall never happen to you" (Matt. 16:22). Grace was cheap in confession but costly in implementation. Peter learned the lesson. If at Caesarea Philippi Peter perceived grace to be cheap, at Rome he demonstrated a more mature understanding in which grace was costly. Peter's personal perspective on grace was best evidenced as a cross was erected for the disciple and he mounted it in the name of Christ.

Costly grace is the means of personal redemption. Both the divine and the human perspectives on grace affirm this truth. Yet, there is more to be said.

Costly grace is the means of personal redemption and the mode of life of the redeemed.

Just as cheap grace is the antithesis of costly grace, so is the life-style derived from cheap grace the exact opposite of the life-style centered upon costly grace. Make no mistake, costly grace is the mode of life of persons who have been redeemed by Jesus Christ.

Cheap grace grants higher priority to occasional verbal confessions of Christ as Lord than to the consistent actional demonstration of Christ's lordship in personal behavior. Evangelists of cheap grace proclaim a discipleship devoid of either disciplines or distinctives and call out converts who need be no diffferent from any one else in society. The gospel of cheap grace focuses upon the blessings of salvation but says little concerning the responsibilities of the saved.

Facilitators of cheap grace talk lucidly about the marvelous possibilities of forgiveness but stop short of any actual implementation of forgiveness in relation to guilt-ridden individuals. Practitioners of cheap grace substitute attendance in church, occasional offerings, and voluntary organizational memberships for a total commitment to Jesus Christ.

A disturbing parable in Matthew 20:1–16 describes how costly grace is to dominate the lives of God's people both in the kingdom of God and in the kingdoms of this world. The story is a startling one.

A landowner sought laborers to work in his vineyard for a day. Four different groups of people were employed. The first group hired was put to work early in the morning. Another group of people was sent to the field a little later in the day and a third group arrived on the job still later in the day. Just before quitting time the employer discovered several individuals who had been merely standing around all day. When he inquired as to why they had not been at work, they responded simply, "No one asked us to work." Of course, they could have exercised some personal initiative, made their way to the field, and requested employment. But, that is not the point. Even though the hour was late and the people seemed apathetic, the landowner put them to work. Thus, at the end of the day some of the laborers had worked long hours, including the hottest part of the day, while others had labored shorter lengths of time. One group had barely done anything before the day ended. When the employer distributed wages for the day, each laborer was paid the same amount.

Few people have difficulty identifying with the reaction of the first three groups: "Look, man, you have done us dirty. True you agreed to pay us a denarius, but at the last hour of the day you brought in all of those scoundrels who did not do much of anything. If you pay them a denarius, you ought to pay us more." The landowner reminded the laborers that he had been true to his agreement with each of them and generous in his provisions.

What is the point? For the laborers, the need for wages was not proportionate to the number of hours worked. Each employee needed a full day's wage. For the employer, the major concern was to meet each laborer's need without acting unjustly toward the others. Thus, "to each according to his need," the concern of grace, replaced "to each according to his due," the principle of justice, as the motivation for action. No person's rights were violated while the needs of all the persons were met. Here is an insight into the nature of God's relationship to his people and into God's expectation for his people's relationship to each other.

The truth of this parable is terribly difficult to accept. Persons who have experienced the grace of God are to live by grace and with grace. Even such ordinary tasks as doing a day's work and paying or collecting the wages related to it are to be pervaded by grace. Life, all of life, is made vulnerable by grace that is costly.

The possibilities of a grace-dominated life are staggering. Think of what could happen in the realm of attitudes.

Common sentiments toward the poor would be reformed. (By "the poor" we usually mean people who possess less than we do.) An affinity to those persons in the parable who worked longest during the day is obvious in the harshness of many contemporary attitudes toward the poor. Frequently heard are comments such as: "These people could do better if they so desired." "There have been times in my life when I had very little but I have done well." "We don't owe the less fortunate anything." and "Most of them are just lazy." A form of justice is involved in this mentality. However, God's people are called to live by grace. Persons are treated according to their needs, not according to what they deserve. Judgment is set aside by grace and condescending pride becomes compassionate ministry.

Prevalent attitudes regarding the affluent would be altered. (By "the affluent" we usually mean people who possess more than we do.) Comments regarding the wealthy are often just as vitriolic as those directed at the poor: "Don't ask me to help those rich people." "They go where they wish and do what they want." "Let them buy whatever assistance they need." "They have far greater financial resources than I will ever have." "There is little I could do for them." and "Frankly, I feel no sense of responsibility toward the wealthy." Again, a distorted kind of justice is involved in such strong feelings. However, again, the point must be made that God's people are to live by grace. A real sensitivity to personal needs is blind to the economics involved. Ministries are performed—a friendly word, understanding, a gesture of friendship—which money cannot buy. Feelings of envy, inferiority, and anger are set aside by grace.

A destructive disposition toward sinners would be changed. (By "sinners" we usually mean people whom we consider to be morally inferior to ourselves.) When someone is in trouble, the voice of cold and calculating justice may say, "That person knew what was involved in the evil act and still chose to participate in it. I have no responsibility to interrupt. Let him live with the consequences of his decision." However, grace—costly grace—demands a different reaction. Justice posits "to each his own." Cheap grace allows for a quick condemnation of the sinner and alleviates any need for help-oriented involvement on the part of anyone. Costly grace is different. It takes its clue from the landowner who provided jobs for the apathetic, and from the father of the prodigal boy who welcomed home his son.

Neither of the parabolic figures greeted a wrongdoer saying, "Live with the consequences. You made your decision. Work it out for yourself." Both spoke the language of grace and demonstrated its generosity.

How different our ordinary days would be if grace were a more common ingredient in them. (That is the way it is supposed to be!) Every aspect of life would be affected—home, church, business, club. Understanding would combat insensitivity, empathy would temper judgmentalness, compassion would muzzle cynicism, and ministry would replace condemnation.

Costly grace is the mode of life of the redeemed.

I remember an occasion when several people had met to contemplate the meaning of grace. Many of the ideas expressed above were verbalized in that situation. After the meeting had adjourned and most of the people had departed, one man remained to talk. He spoke as if he could not believe what he had heard and his words took the form of a question: "Do you know what would happen if I really believed that what you have said is true and if tomorrow I began to live like that?" "Yes, I do," I responded. The gentleman walked away shaking his head, sobered by the need and staggered by the possibilities of a life lived by costly grace.

Costly grace is the means of personal redemption and the mode of life of the redeemed.

Christianity In Work Clothes

"Six days you shall labor, and do all your work;"

Exodus 20:9

> *"God is living, working still,*
> *All things work and move;*
> *Work, or lose the power to will,*
> *Lose the power to love."*
>
> JOHN SULLIVAN DWIGHT

7
Christianity In Work Clothes

By the time most people reach the age for retirement they have invested approximately 125,000 hours of their lives in work. That statistic is true for all who devote a minimum of forty hours per week to their jobs or to preparation for their jobs.[1] Add to this astonishing fact the observation of a perceptive student of the American way of life: "The majority of adults in this country hate their work. . . . For most Americans, work is mindless, exhausting, boring, servile . . . something to be endured."[2]

Viewed from an entirely secular perspective, work may be seen as a necessary evil which holds all except the most elite within its grip. However, there is an alternative.

The all-pervasive phenomenon of work takes on profound significance when held up to the light of Scripture and Christian doctrine. Through the ages, the people of God have devoted a great deal of attention to the responsibilities of labor. Consistent with other interpretations of the ordinary involvements of life, Christians understand work in relation to the lordship of Jesus Christ. This theological alternative to a secular evaluation of work encourages faithful Christian discipleship among believers who spend their days in business suits, uniforms, coveralls, and other types of work clothes.

Work is a blessing.

People have for too long been burdened by the old myth that work is a curse. Some biblical interpreters persist in propagating the idea that labor is a product of the fall of man. Advocates of this position explain that people have to toil in order to make a living because of sin. Such a negative view of work fails to reflect the truth of the Bible.

According to the creation accounts of Genesis, work is a blessing not a curse. Labor is not to be understood as a continuous means of punishment for Adam's sin but as an ongoing gift willed by God from the very beginning. Genesis 1:28 describes God's twofold blessing for his newly-formed creatures—procreation and work. Furthermore, Genesis 2:15, which still precedes the account of the fall of man, states, "God took the man and put him in the Garden of Eden to till it and keep it."

God himself is a working God. A recurring theme throughout the Bible is "the works of God." Creation itself is described in Genesis as an act of work—"And on the seventh day God finished his work" (2:2); "So God blessed the seventh day and hallowed it, because on it God rested from all his work which he had done in creation" (2:3). Since God is a working God and human beings were created "in the image of God," it is only natural that every individual, like the Creator, exists as a working being.

After the fall of man, sin caused a change in people, not their work. Work was still a legitimate gift from God but sin affected the human attitude toward this gift. What God had intended as a blessing and looked upon as good, people saw as a curse and accepted as evil. Governed by such feelings, the stringent demands of work became a drudgery and participation in labor led to deadly fatigue. However, note carefully that the problem is with people, not with work.

When understood as it was intended, work is accepted as

humankind's part in helping God transform the world. That is to say, creation is not finished. God is still at work in the world and we are called upon to join our efforts to the divine activity. When a person's labors result in constructive change, that individual participates fully in the true character of work.

Obviously, such an interpretation of work seems more compatible with some jobs than with others. The farmer who tills the soil, plants the seed, and harvests the grain has little difficulty viewing himself as a partner with God in creation. The social worker who devotes a majority of her time to rehabilitative efforts has no trouble sensing the essence of work as change when she observes minds broadened, living conditions improved, and the quality of life so radically altered that scowling frowns become pleasant smiles. However, though the immediacy of recognition may vary, all true work participates in such a transformation of the world.

Here is an individual on an assembly line who for eight hours each day with boring repetition turns out the same screw. Here is a salesperson who spends days away from family and friends in an effort to sell one particular industrial tool. Laborers and tasks such as these, which can be multiplied a thousand times, may seem to provide exceptions to the high view of work discussed above. Not so.

These are people whose tasks must be seen against the backdrop of a larger finished product—a communications instrument vital to the news media, an ocean liner or an airplane forming an integral link in the growing chain of international transportation systems, a kidney machine which saves a life, a house which takes a family off the streets. In their work, regardless of how minor their roles in the finished product, they help mold the shape of the world.

Another ingredient in the biblical view of work as blessing merits recognition. All work is to be related to

God's call. In the thought of the Bible, all people share the same calling though individual functions in society may differ. Calling is a theological term; function is a sociological one. God's call to every person is the same—accept the lordship of Christ and become an agent in his ministry of redemption. Ministry in Christ's name constitutes the Christian's vocation.[3]

The manner in which Christians make a living and serve society should be decided in light of God's call. The only restrictions are that the labor serve in some way to meet a need and that it be of such a nature as not to demoralize or dehumanize the persons involved. Paul's vocation was that of an ambassador for Christ; at times he sewed tents to make a living.

When work is so understood, there is no double standard of value between a sacred job and a secular job. An individual may effectively serve God and participate in his ministry of redemption while working at a so-called "secular" job or while serving in what is known as a "sacred" job. Participants in neither are to feel that they are inherently better or more important merely because of their position. In reality, secular work is made religious and religious work is made secular in the all-embracing concept of vocation as the ministry of redemption.

Work is service.

A second major idea embraced by a Christian view of work is that work is basically service. It is service to God and to people.

Consider the example of Jesus. The years prior to his public ministry were spent in a little carpentry shop in Nazareth. Week by week Jesus remained at home giving himself to the traditional labor of his family until one of the younger family members could assume the responsibility.

Once Jesus departed from the workbench in his hometown and moved through the baptismal waters of the Jordan and the arid regions of the desert where he was tempted, he embarked upon a public ministry devoted to service. Taking upon himself the role of the Messiah as depicted by Isaiah in terms of a Suffering Servant, Jesus ministered to people by meeting both their physical and spiritual needs. Thus, service was neither a postscript nor an idealistic luxury for Jesus. It was the entirety of his way of life.

Work for Christians has a purpose and that purpose is service. In some tasks and on some days the service-oriented nature of labor is more readily apparent than at other times. Obviously, situations develop in which work becomes a pain in the neck, when the monotony of an everyday labor routine drives one almost to the point of insanity. However, there are also other moments in which labor takes on great meaning and when physical fatigue is accompanied by a feeling of accomplishment. Whether interpreted in terms of immediate benefits or long-range implications, expenditures of energy in a daily task are related to the attainment of worthy goals or the accomplishment of noble purposes.

Work is limited.

Any discussion of a biblical-Christian perspective on work is incomplete apart from the assertion that work is to be limited. Work is not all there is to life.

Just as work was a part of God's intention in creation, so was rest. In fact, work and rest are equal components of creation. Rest is far more than an interruption of labor or a weakling's diversion from labor. Rest is a necessary ingredient in the life of one committed to genuinely creative work. Even God himself had to rest and he declared as "holy" the day of rest.

Here is a word of fundamental importance to our work-saturated society. Work is not an end in itself. The Bible's teaching on the importance of rest calls into question any philosophy which measures success only in terms of the accumulation of goods. It is a hasty judgment which posits that those who fail to work constantly are lazy and without worth, a stereotype evaluation of sitting in idleness as a waste of time.

Manual labor is to be balanced by an exercise of the mind. Contemplation complements all of the other activities of life. A major tragedy in this activistic society is erosion in the quality of being affected by citizens' preoccupation with the importance of doing. Contemporaries can point with pride to contributions of skyscrapers, rapid transit systems, industrial cybernation, and mechanical gadgets, but are hard pressed to think of a single recent contribution made to the spirits of people. In truth, the aesthetic aspects of life are as important as the physical.

God forbid that we build cities for people to inhabit, assign them jobs to do, provide them meetings to attend, fill their stomachs at company picnics, and starve their souls. Amidst all of the great works produced by a proliferation of action-oriented agendas, we must recover the poetry which once filled human lives as the gift of God. Already we can observe the sad result of altercations in human nature which have desensitized the human spirit—individuals who can be distracted from the beauty of a sunset by the roar of a jet engine!

Communion and enjoyment in personal experience—essential elements if there is to be life rather than mere existence—are threatened when an individual ignores the need for rest and allows spirituality to become stagnant. Jesus' visit to the house of his friends Mary and Martha demonstrated the significance of this truth. In vain, Jesus spoke to Martha about how sitting and listening can sometimes be more important than stirring among pots and pans. Martha missed the point. Like so many other people, she was so busy about her chores that she missed an opportunity for a unique experience with the Lord.

Preservation of society is partially dependent upon a rediscovery of the importance of community and a genuine sense of enjoyment. Being must become as important as doing, and resting as mandatory as working. Within the fellowship of such common life-styles, work can be saved from an attitude which desires something for nothing and realized as a blessing to be used in service to others.

Several years ago I worked for an entire summer with an elderly member of a small rural church which I served as pastor. This gentleman did heavy farm labor for twelve to fourteen hours everyday of the week except Sunday. My parishioner and his wife lived in a one-hundred-year-old house furnished for them by his employer, a wealthy bank executive. The man's salary was $3.00 per day. He earned an extra $2.00 a day when he fed the cattle both morning and evening.

In the early fall of that year I conducted the funeral of this friend. Knowledge of the dedication which he brought to his work, the strenuous tasks to which he gave himself, and the sparse wages which were his to keep temporarily, left a bad impression with me. Dominant, however, is my sense of awe regarding the spirit of this individual. He did not complain. In fact, his attitude was positive and his disposition contagiously cheerful. Perhaps the reason was that he had come to see his work as all work is meant to be seen—it is done for man but it is offered to God.

The Atheist Within

"I believe; help my unbelief!"

Mark 9:24

*"An atheist's laugh's a poor exchange
For Deity offended!"*

ROBERT BURNS

8
The Atheist Within

The statement "I don't believe in God!" has long been the most reprehensible confession of human concoction. Biblical writers were unfamiliar with deniers of God. In fact, the Scriptures display no cognizance of arguments which dispute God's existence. Historically, atheists have been considered dangerous and their beliefs labeled as heresy. Presently, questionable legal statutes prevent atheists from holding some government offices in various parts of the United States. Atheism is a philosophy abhorred by most people who understand it and feared by many who cannot comprehend its meaning.

Usually the term *atheist* is applied to an individual who has hypothesized and perhaps even confessed that there is no God. However, the word is also applicable to persons who ignore, if not deny, the existence of God by their actions. Cerebral rejection of the existence of a sovereign God is characteristic of theoretical atheists. Behavioral refutation of the existence of a sovereign God is the unholy witness of practical atheists. God may be denied by people's actions as well as by their lips.

Practical atheism is certainly more prevalent than theoretical atheism, and it may well be more dangerous. A respectable national survey revealed that 94 percent of the people in the United States confess a belief in God.[1] Yet a similar study aimed at finding the percentage of these same people whose lives exert a pervasive influence in private and social morals would most likely produce a much smaller figure. Practical atheists believe in God but do not worship and serve God. They extol God as Creator but exploit his creation, acknowledge God as universal Judge but ignore the importance of personal accountability, and praise God as Redeemer but refuse to live the life of the redeemed. Some behavioral deniers of God even assume the title of Christian for purposes of religious identity while giving no evidence of a commitment to Christ's lordship in matters of religious activity.

In a very real sense theoretical atheists take God more seriously than do their practical counterparts. Intellectual denials of God are often the result of prolonged and serious struggles to determine that which stands at the center of life and is relevant to all around it. Because of shortsightedness, a preoccupation with the scientific method of documentation, a distrust of any nonmaterial reality, or some other reason, the presence of God is rejected as a possibility. Practical atheists passively assume the existence of God, thoughtlessly relegate his presence to the periphery of life, and foolishly estimate that his eternal will is totally irrelevant to contemporary decisions.

An interesting story is told regarding a conversation between Rabbi Nahman and a young man who came to him defiantly but anxiously proclaiming a disbelief in God. The Rabbi's initial response was: "So, you don't believe in God; why get so excited about it? If God does not exist, it can't be very important, can it?" Retaining his mood of severity, the unbeliever protested: "Rabbi, how can you talk that way? It is important; it's the most important thing in the world."[2] That is the point! A theoretical atheist may be closer to genuine commitment to God than the practical atheist who never gives a serious thought to God and his will.

A deeply disturbing dimension of this whole matter is that something of the practical atheist constantly seeks to be born in all of us. What I have in mind is not an outright atheistic orientation to life as a whole but an atheistic perspective on a particular part of life—perhaps some personal desire, goal, or activity. This is the "atheist within."

The atheist within a person attempts to bracket off a segment of that individual's life and quarantine this realm from any contact with God. Though confessions of divine sovereignty and testimonies of eternal salvation persist in all other aspects of life, one area of existence is devoid of any recognition of God's presence. At this single point a person will not let God be God. In this one realm of life, a person acts as if God did not exist. Such is the abode and the posture of the atheist within.

Practical atheism promises an evil plight.

No better description of the life of the practical atheist is to be found than that offered by the author of Psalm 14. Commenting on this piece of literature, J. R. P. Sclater observed: "The core of the psalm is . . . a statement of the spiritual state of the practical atheist and his inevitable history of futility and fear."[3] Recognition of the truth that a potential for practical atheism exists in every person adds importance to learning what the psalmist teaches about the evil plight of those who deny God. Look how life fares for the practical atheist—the individual who harbors an atheist within.

Immediately apparent among practical atheists is the fact that "they are corrupt, they do abominable deeds" (Ps. 14:1). Operative is the law of an inclined plane. Apart from any reference to God, people find themselves more and more involved in attitudes and activities which destroy life rather than nurture it. One evil deed which seems insignificant leads to another immoral act of more significance and that to yet another form of corruption. Divorced from consistent contemplation of God's will, people lose their moral sensitivity and become apathetic about evil. Life slides steadily downward. Practical atheists confront few forms of behavior which shock them or even disturb them. Soon they lose any ability to blush in shame.

The same phenomenon characterizes the particular work of the atheist within as marks the general posture of explicit practical atheism. To isolate one aspect of life from God is to create a condition in which corruption grows and spreads like a rapid cancer. When any single segment of life is segregated from the divine will, the evil in that sector spills over into other sectors of life and delivers its deadly infection.

Without a recognition of God which evokes repentance, a second dimension of practical atheism inevitably follows "the abominable deeds." The psalmist described it this way: "They have all gone astray, they are all alike corrupt; there is none that does good no, not one" (Ps. 14:3). At this point actions have begun adversely to affect being. Deeds of evil done almost thoughtlessly have turned in upon the individuals involved and poisoned the entirety of their lives. The King James translators stated the situation graphically in their rendering of this passage—"they are altogether become filthy."

That one domain of life over which the practical atheist has retained control for selfish purposes eventually alters all of life. Because of an attempt to master one division of existence apart from God, with no real harm intended, a person discovers the self in servitude to an evil which has taken over all of existence in defiance to God, and great harm ensues. The situation is serious. Attempts to live as if God does not exist stop short of magnificent self-exaltation and joyous self-indulgence. Life becomes marred down in utter filth and despair.

The final development in the evil plight of the practical atheist is the neglect of God in specific acts of personal behavior and this consequent poisoning of a person's entire nature begins to destroy relationships with other people (Ps. 14:4–6). God can be ignored so frequently that an individual can take advantage of others with little thought given to anything except selfish gain. Both the rights and the needs of acquaintances are disregarded. Any negative twinge of conscience regarding the individual's despicable treatment of others is quickly excused by reasoning that the "others" are members of an inferior race or a different social class unworthy of concern. The road is not long from practical atheism to the kind of pagan treatment of human beings evidenced around the gas chambers of Auschwitz, in the riot-torn streets of some of our cities, and among the unjust practices of prejudice disguised as institutional policy. To travel that road is to walk into hell!

Depersonalizing relationships produces a pervasive fear. No one individual trusts any other individual. All live under the heavy burden imposed by dread, anxiety, and suspicion.

Of particular interest is the psalmist's comment, "You would confound the plans of the poor, but the Lord is his refuge" (Ps. 14:6). What a terrible indictment. Practical atheists conduct themselves in a manner intended to intimidate those who live by a simple faith in God. Persons who casually relate to God and take life in their own hands tend to disparage those who take God seriously and live only for him. Individuals who recklessly abandon any consideration of the divine will seem to seek a supportive camaraderie of evil as together they shake their fists in the faces of people who live by faith.

Practical atheism promises an evil plight. The end is not good for those who harbor an atheist within. Practical atheism grows and spreads and poisons. Practical atheists sooner or later end up fighting within themselves as well as with their neighbors. Even more tragically, by both attitudes and actions they set themselves apart from the only source which can give help.

Despite the gloom produced by a consideration of practical atheism, the psalmist concluded his observations with a note of hope (Ps. 14:7). He looked forward to the coming Messiah who would challenge any attitude in conflict with God's sovereignty and call people to the kind of life in which practical atheism would be no more. We join in that hope with the realization that that promise has now become fulfilled.

Practical atheism is challenged by Christ's call to discipleship and destroyed by Christ's redemptive presence.

Jesus provides no salvation for people who maintain a selfish mastery over one aspect of life. Either God matters infinitely or he does not really matter at all. Jesus Christ is either the most important person in all of creation, or he is not important at all. Faith is of like manner. Redemptive faith in Christ penetrates every component of a person's life and silences any atheistic voice within. Where genuine faith in Christ is present, all of life is faithful to Christ.

The call to Christian discipleship is meant to reveal, challenge, and destroy every pocket of practical atheism in an individual's life. Even as Jesus invited people to follow him, he admonished them to count the cost of this followship before making a positive response. No vestige of atheism could be tolerated. Christ wanted the entirety of life committed to his leadership. Warnings of stringent demands stood side by side with promises of unparalleled blessings in

Jesus' summons to salvation. Consider some of his representative comments:

He who is not with me is against me (Matt. 12:30).

If any man would come after me, let him deny himself and take up his cross daily and follow me (Luke 9:23).

He who loves father or mother more than me is not worthy of me; and he who loves son or daughter more than me is not worthy of me; and he who does not take his cross and follow me is not worthy of me (Matt. 10:37–38).

Numerous Gospel stories convey the intensity of Jesus' attack upon practical atheism. Time after time Jesus challenged and sought to destroy tendencies toward atheism in the life of a potential disciple. Luke (9:57–62) relates a trilogy of such experiences which is instructive.

On one occasion an individual approached Jesus boldly volunteering to follow him anywhere. Surprisingly Jesus responded to the man's offer with a warning rather than with a statement of acceptance. When the discomforts of discipleship were described, the man's enthusiasm waned; and he turned away. The atheist within this individual had a mind for comfort. He did not necessarily demand luxury, but he did desire a good place in which to rest comfortably at night. This person would follow Jesus if only he could retain control of where he slept and ate. Jesus would have none of that. Discipleship could not embrace even a subtle atheism—desires over which Jesus was not allowed to be Lord.

Two other individuals attempted a conditional acceptance of Jesus' call to discipleship. Both registered an intention to follow Christ, but each had a pressing responsibility to which top priority had been assigned. Jesus sternly rebuked their atheistic attitude. A decision had to be made. Jesus was either important enough to be followed immediately or he was not important enough to be followed at all. No demand could take precedence over his. Discipleship must contain no hint of a denial of Christ, no trace of atheism.

Anyone who wishes to stand in the saving presence of God's grace must allow God's grace to infiltrate every segment of life and dissolve any fragment of atheism. We cannot follow Christ in all ways except one. We either follow him in all ways or we do not really follow him.

For some people the atheist within wears a business suit. These persons are exemplary Christians except for their economic endeavors. The feeling is that too much risk is involved in an application of the teachings of Christ to the economic realm. Since their competitors may operate by the law of the jungle, these individuals feel they must be prepared for anything and act as success-oriented needs dictate. Accumulation, conservation, and expenditures of money are "purely financial" concerns.

In the lives of other people, the atheist within is preoccupied with pleasure. Based upon the conclusion that pleasure is a necessity, these individuals have reserved for themselves the right to define the boundaries of pleasure. Consequently, the pursuit of pleasure may conflict with responsibilities related to one's family, church, and friends, or even push one beyond behavior acceptable in terms of Christian morality.

Still other people encounter the atheist within as they confront a detrimental habit. Their rationale is: "I know that this habit is morally questionable and physically harmful. However, this is the only activity of this nature in which I indulge. People will understand." Interpreted from a biblical perspective such reasoning means: "I will not permit God to enter this sector of my life. I will live in this realm as if he did not exist."

Any time people look deep within themselves discoveries are made of areas which seem fertile for the development of atheism. We may say little about these aspects of life but they are there. Domains exist in which we seek to live as if God were not alive—in family relations, in fits of anger, in jealous retaliation, in sexual manipulation, in social snobbery, in racial prejudice, in political involvements, in financial stewardship, in religious witness.

An authentic response to Christ's challenging call is radical in nature. Persons either make an unconditional commitment of their lives to Christ or offer an admission that some form of practical atheism lingers within them. Salvation and deliverance are the results of the former response while death in isolation is the end of the latter.

Practical atheism promises an evil plight. However, practical atheism is challenged by Christ's call to discipleship and destroyed by Christ's redemptive presence. The good news of the gospel is that all people may come to know the joy of living in Christ and the peace of having God in control of all of life.

In the presence of Christ atheism is dead!

The Near Ends of God

"And the Lord said, 'Behold, there is a place by me where you shall stand upon the rock; and while my glory passes by I will put you in a cleft of the rock, and I will cover you with my hand until I have passed by; then I will take away my hand, and you shall see my back; but my face shall not be seen!' "

Exodus 33:21–23

"So nigh is grandeur to our dust,
So near is God to man,"

RALPH WALDO EMERSON

9
The Near Ends Of God

"If you are God, reveal yourself to me!" was Moses' bold challenge to his Creator. "Show me thy glory" (Ex. 33:18) were his words. As audacious as that may seem, let us not be too hard on Moses and too quick to condemn him. In reality, Moses gave voice to a gnawing heartfelt longing shared by scores of people.

Out of the anguish of his sufferings Job cried, "Let the Almighty answer me!" (Job 31:35). Seeking to resolve the dilemma of ambivalent beliefs, the scribes and Pharisees said to Jesus, "Teacher, we wish to see a sign from you" (Matt. 12:38). An honest seeker of meaningful religion confesses, "How much easier it would be if God would just do some great act and let me know he was behind it." A shy and frequently hesitant Christian explains, "I would probably be much bolder in my witness and I would certainly be more devoted to my faith if God would only make himself better known to me." From Moses' time to the present, numerous are the persons who have thought, "My convictions would be stronger and my life-style more moral if God would reveal himself to me in a dramatic way."

Moses wanted an absolute revelation from God. He desired to know all there was to know about God, to strip away the mystery, to penetrate the holiness, to stare at the divine countenance. Such exposure would never be a part of

Moses' experience, however, just as it will never be a reality in the life of any person. By his very nature, the infinite God cannot be fully comprehended by finite human beings. The biblical account of Moses' dialogue with God about this matter in Exodus 33:18–23 is both interesting and instructive.

As a response to Moses' demand for a divine disclosure comes the announcement that neither Moses nor any other person can see God's face and live. Moses will have to be content to view only the back of God, "the hind parts of God."[1]

Humankind is unable to comprehend the totality of God—to plumb the depths of his holiness and to span the breadth of his transcendence. Yet, no individual can be completely devoid of any knowledge of God. The presence of God touches all persons at some point. Those sensitive to the divine revelation catch at least a glimpse of God, usually only a quick glance at his back.

Actually, problems exist in knowing how even to communicate about God in a meaningful manner. God's nature is far greater than any description of it. His essence cannot be reduced to a single word. The divine character defies delimitation by any one analogy. An individual's yearning for the divine presence is certainly not satisfied by the presentation of an abstraction, regardless of how holy it may seem. People will not give themselves to a generality. No one can love a proposition.

Of course, the good news of the Bible is that people searching for God do not have to settle for only faint knowledge of an abstract generalization. Always present is the kind of revelation which Moses referred to as the back of God, that which can be called the near ends of God.

Harry Emerson Fosdick spoke helpfully to this point as he

developed a moving analogy of an individual's relationship to God. Said Fosdick, "Now I do not know the whole sea. It is very great. . . . Wide areas of the sea are to me unknown, but I know the sea. It has a near end. It washes my island. I can sit beside it and bathe in it and sail over it and be sung to sleep by the music of it."[2] Then came the insightful interpretation. "So is God. He is so great that in his vastness we can think of him only in symbolic terms, but he has a near end. Indeed, the nub of the whole inquiry about the nature of Deity lies in the answer to this question: Where do we think in our experience we touch the near end of God?"[3]

Fosdick's question gives rise to other questions and points the way to mature faith. What about the near end of God? Where can we meet him? How do we come to know him?

Of necessity, words and thoughts regarding God are paradoxical. God is awesomely transcendent and lovingly eminent. He is so different from any other person as to seem totally unapproachable and yet so intimately involved with all persons as to be invitingly approachable. God can be experienced by everyone everywhere and at every time yet known individually in specific places and at definite times. Almighty God is known by the near ends of his existence.

Once all of that has been stated, more questions come surging to the forefront. What constitutes the near end of God? When, where, and how can God be encountered? Are there places, acts, or people so holy as to reveal the being of God? Are these the near ends of God?

The near ends of God include creation, the moral order, worship experiences, the church, and people.

Some people discern the presence of God by means of his creation. The psalmist traced his thoughts about the relationship between God the Creator and man the creature directly to sources in nature—

> When I look at thy heavens, the
> work of thy fingers,
> The moon and the stars which thou
> hast established (Ps. 8:3).

Job also discovered the near end of God in the created order—

> But ask the beasts, and they will teach you;
> The birds of the air, and they will tell you;
> or the plants of the earth, and they will teach you;
> and the fish of the sea will declare to you.
> Who among all these does not know
> that the hand of the Lord has done this? (Job 12:7–9)

Another psalm sounds the same refrain even more explicitly—

> The heavens are telling the glory of God;
> and the firmament proclaims his handiwork.
> Day to day pours forth speech,
> and night to night declares knowledge. (Ps. 19:1–2)

Persons in more recent times have had similar experiences. A despairing individual has found hope in the coming of spring. At the end of a sleepless night, one mired up in self-pity and perplexed by personal difficulties discovered a new dimension of help in the beauty of a sunrise. Tired minds, aching bodies, and troubled spirits more than once have discovered new life during a long walk along the beach, peering off a mountain summit into the green foliage of fertile valleys, or picking a bouquet of fresh flowers. A snowfall, a bush aflame with autumn colors, and raindrops splashing in mud puddles all have the potential to help a person hear God speak, feel his presence, or sense his nature.

Occasionally persons encounter the near end of God in confrontation with the reality of a moral order. Basic ethical principles which have been intellectually examined in hypothetical situations are finally learned in actual personal experiences. Life confirms in numerous specific events what the Bible teaches in passage after passage. Sure enough, people do reap what they sow in terms of good and evil.

"The wages of sin is death" (Rom. 6:23). Fruits of a life selfishly invested include "immorality, impurity, licentiousness, idolatry, sorcery, enmity, strife, jealousy, anger, selfishness, dissension, party spirit, envy, drunkenness, carousing, and the like" (Gal. 5:19–21). Evil sets people on an incline and life slides steadily downward. Immorality is destructive—either immediately or ultimately.

"Blessed are those who hunger and thirst after righteousness" (Matt. 5:6). Fruits of a life devoted to what God requires of people—"to do justice, and to love kindness, and to walk humbly with your God" (Micah 6:8)—include "love, joy, peace, patience, kindness, goodness, faithfulness, gentleness, self control" (Gal. 5:22). The doing of good creates an environment in which genuine growth can take place. Righteousness is triumphant—either immediately or ultimately.

Realizations of the moral order grow out of differing circumstances:

> A young man seeks pleasure in all the wrong places and in all the wrong ways. Finally, in a situation of absolute misery, he cries out for help. Waiting for assistance, he catches a glimpse of God.
>
> A group of people commit themselves to work for equally distributed justice in their community. After discouragement, setbacks, threats, punishment, and fatigue, they are ready to quit. Then, when least ex-

pected, they see justice done, discern the presence of God, and find the strength to continue their work

After flaunting a mindless and heartless exploitative attitude toward business associates, a woman finds herself shamefully exploited. The reality of what she has done dawns, a plea for forgiveness is uttered, and she senses something of the nature of God.

Persons who reject every form of discipline, seek to settle all disputes by mental or physical violence, and measure success in terms of winning may see the near end of God when they find themselves decimated by the kind of ruthless materialism which they have encouraged and when they admit their need for an alternate life-style.

A lady committed to verbal, intellectual, and relational integrity is almost overcome by temptations to compromise honesty in each of these realms. In finding the courage to be faithful to her convictions, she discovers the moral resourcefulness of God.

Persons reaching out for spiritual help, desperately seeking forgiveness, pursuing justice, and grasping for moral courage frequently run headlong into the near end of God.

For numerous persons a service of corporate worship has been the "cleft of the rock" from which the near end of God has been witnessed. An individual becomes a part of a congregation so intent upon meeting the Holy One that the worshipers' silence is disturbingly stark but encouragingly vibrant. One voice is joined to another and those to others in loud exaltation as God is praised and in somber penitence as sins are confessed. A thrill rushes through the lives of those who listen to the assurance of forgiveness. Good news is proclaimed from the pulpit and pondered by all "who have ears to hear." A sense of humility, a twinge of excitement, and a surge of gratitude accompany the realization that a divine invitation has been extended to every member of the congregation. In worship, God in his glory passes by.

Of course, not every occasion for worship will equal Isaiah's life-transforming experience in the Temple or Ezekiel's dramatic vision of assurance by the river Chebar. Often we may gather and depart having seen no smoke and heard no angels. Even during these times, however, God's presence can be real and close. Lives have reached out and touched the near end of God.

The church is the near end of God. Within the fellowship of believers one may participate in a continuation of the love which became incarnate in Jesus Christ. Here is a fellowship of healing—troubled minds are therapeutically counseled, fractured spirits are nurtured toward wholeness, diseased bodies are put in touch with healing medicines, broken relationships are pointed toward reconciliation. Here is a fellowship of proclamation—the good news of salvation is heralded, divine judgment upon sin is announced, moral perspectives on social issues are discussed, basic principles of the Christian life are enunciated. Here is a fellowship of prayer—for blessings received and sins committed, for individuals and institutions, for fellow believers and those who do not know redemption, for private pursuits and public policies. Here is a fellowship of ministry—to spiritual needs and physical needs, to hungering souls and starving stomachs, to inquisitive minds and troubled hearts, to all who need help. Where lives touch the fellowship of the church they become acquainted with the near end of God.

Some persons find the near end of God in the life of another person. Indicative of this truth are well-worn characterizations such as "There is a saintly man" and "She surely is a godly woman." Both are compliments to individuals whose lives are transparent to God. To observe these people is to be enlightened regarding the nature of God.

A caring woman comes to a family in crisis, listens to the members with concern, counsels them lovingly, ministers to them responsibly, and becomes for those involved the near end of God.

A contemporary good Samaritan rescues abused individuals, attends their wounds, and seeks to correct the conditions which could inflict a similar harm on others. Some of the persons helped no doubt believe they have benefited from a divine visitation.

That person who exercises faith, receives strength from hope, and unselfishly lives as a servant gives others an insight into what God is like.

*The near ends of God invite exploration
into the fullness of God.*

Misunderstanding must be avoided. More remains to be said. The near ends of God do not provide complete knowledge about God. They reveal a part of the divine glory but not all of it. Within them there is profound insight and from them there is helpful inspiration. However, they point toward something more.

To encounter the near ends of God is to be invited to explore the fullness of God. Channels into the Holy are opened not closed. Once my stance is secure at water's edge, where the ocean first touches the beach, I am ready to take another step forward, a step into deeper water, a step which entrusts more of my being to the depths of the ocean. So it is in experiencing God. Contact with a near end of God places one securely on the edge, in a position to pursue the God who has been found and to discover God's pursuit of all who are lost. An even greater commitment to God is the appropriate and likely response.

What happens in a continuing exploration of God is strange and beautiful. Intrigue with God's vastness is soon transformed into awareness of his nearness. Wonder at God's involvement in the spectacular is complemented by awe at his presence in the ordinary. That which is seen of God in creation that provokes appreciation leads finally to that which is known about God personally that provokes commitment. That which is revealed about God through the moral order points toward the incarnation of God in Jesus Christ, who lived the ethic which he taught. That which is learned about God in unique moments of worship draws people into a relationship with God which sanctifies every moment and makes every place a holy place. That which is seen of God in the loving fellowship of the church summons one to the source of the love and fellowship. That which is discovered about God in another person causes one ultimately to look at the Christ in whom God was most fully present.

Though the near ends of God attract, inform, and inspire us, they never completely satisfy us. Each run-in with God beckons us to a more complete knowledge of God and thus to a redemptive encounter with Christ. In Jesus of Nazareth we stand before the perfect revelation of God. Jesus is the near end of God but more. New Testament witnesses said, "He is the image of the invisible God" (Col. 1:15) and "in him all the fullness of God was pleased to dwell" (Col. 1:19).

Pursuit of the near ends of God leads finally to Christ. In him is salvation—knowledge about God gives way to a knowledge of God. The God of the ages becomes a personal God. Reverence and respect remain, but these responses to God are joined by everlasting love. The God who is beyond all people comes to live in every individual who will accept him. He who is Creator and Sustainer, Alpha and Omega, is known also as Redeemer. With Christ as Savior, anyone may approach the omnipotent, omniscient, omnipresent God and call him Father!

Make no mistake at this point. Once all of the above has been written about, thought about, and spoken about, the subject is not exhausted. God is inexhaustible. There will always be more to know about God than is presently known. Any relationship with him can be deepened substantially. God offers a constant challenge and a never-ending hope.

Christians properly continue to reach out for the near ends of God and appropriately follow these. We daily try to give ourselves to God anew—venturing further into his being and growing in his likeness. As a result, we dare to live in such a manner that we might become for someone else the near ends of God!

For Everything A Season

"For everything there is a season, and a time for every matter under heaven."

Ecclesiastes 3:1

"When a man takes an oath . . . he's holding his own self in his own hands. Like water . . .
And if he opens his fingers then—*he needn't hope to find himself again."*

ROBERT BOLT

10
For Everything A Season

> For everything there is a season,
> and a time for every matter under heaven:
> a time to be born, and a time to die;
> a time to plant, and a time to pluck
> up what is planted;
> a time to kill, and a time to heal;
> a time to break down, and a time to
> build up;
> a time to weep, and a time to laugh;
> a time to mourn, and a time to dance;
> a time to cast away stones, and a
> time to gather stones together;
> a time to embrace, and a time to
> refrain from embracing;
> a time to seek, and a time to lose;
> a time to keep, and a time to cast
> away;
> a time to rend, and a time to sew;
> a time to keep silence, and a time to
> speak;
> a time to love, and a time to hate;
> a time for war, and a time for peace.
> (Eccl. 3:1–8)

What a chronicle of human experiences! But what is the

purpose? What is the intent of these words—to emphasize the value of clocks and schedules, to elucidate the practical moral axiom about seizing a time when you find it, to outline the orderly existence of lives predestined by a God who foreordains some? Maybe this is merely an observation of the way things really are.

Most students of the Scriptures agree that in the writer's mind were thoughts of predestination. The author of this literature reveals a pervasive pessimism, almost a rank bitterness at times. His is the constant refrain:
"Vanity of vanities . . . vanity of vanities! All is vanity." (Eccl. 1:2).

The view of time and history expounded in Ecclesiastes incorporates all personal experiences into a cyclical movement. The episodes of an individual's life are made analogous to the predictable revolvement of the seasons. As there is a time for summer and a time for winter so there is a time to embrace and a time to refrain from embracing. However, there is more to be learned from "the preacher's" message than merely this rigidly-patterned, negatively-oriented view of time and history.

The wisdom of this Old Testament book must be set in the broader context of the entire biblical message. Reflection on the words of Koheleth should be in remembrance of a deeper knowledge which comes out of that body of literature provoked by the life of Christ.

Notice how important balance is in human development.

So imperative is balance that one needed experience may be contingent upon another experience. There is a time for giving one's self away—to a marital partner, in an act of service on behalf of people in need, for a purpose which appears even more important than life itself. However, the phenomenon of self-giving is dependent upon proper self-understanding. An individual must come to grips with who he or she is in such a manner that the self *can* be given away.

There is a time for reaping. But what if there has been no season of planting? Harvests will not come automatically. Neither in the realm of agriculture nor in the spiritual life of a church will the season of harvest be completely different from the season of planting. If a farmer does not plant corn in the spring, he does not expect to find an abundant stand of corn in his fields turned tan by the coming of fall. Likewise, a church can expect no discrepancy, no discontinuity between that which it sows at seedtime and that which it reaps at harvesttime. A person concerned about the present and the future must take a long look at what has been invested in order to make the present what it is and the future what it will be.

The tedious nature inherent in a proper balance of seasons is also evident in the fact that one experience may be destructive apart from another experience of an entirely different nature. Wholeness involves more than one season.

There is a time to work and a time to refrain from working. For any person to work constantly apart from rest is for that individual to choose a course of destruction. Demolished along the way will be families, spirituality, and perhaps even the worker's life. However, a constant relaxation may be as destructive as never-ending labor. Devoid of any exercise, muscles grow weak, mental faculties deteriorate, and a person loses a sense of significance regarding life. Ecclesiastes is right—the totality of life need not be either work or rest. Wholeness involves both.

There is a time to build up and a time to tear down, a time to be supportive and a time to be critical, a time to soar with ideals and a time to trudge with reality. Yet, suffering results when a person becomes locked into any one of these experiences, and decides upon one as a style of life devoid of the others.

How the importance of balance needs to be understood by church people. There is a time for emphasizing exclusiveness—for focusing on a local church family, for being almost totally concerned about a specific community—but there is a time to emphasize commonality—a bond of fellowship, an identity with all who call Christ Lord. People can become so involved in reaching out their arms to those around them that they fail to embrace some needy folks within their own church family. Likewise, individuals can become so narrowly engrossed in their own kind of people that they never experience the joy of relationships in the larger body of Christ.

Again, there is a time to be silent and a time to speak; a time to listen and a time to talk. No person can speak on every single issue of importance never indulging in the practice of silent study without it soon becoming obvious that the individual is suffering from a lack of balance and is without any real competence to speak on anything. This principle holds true for both the pastor of a congregation and for every member of a church fellowship. Times of proclamation and declaration simply must be preceded by times of meditation and study.

Only occasionally do situations arise when a person of conscience must speak immediately. At these times, as homespun philosophers have pointed out, silence tends to be more yellow than golden. Harold Bosley offered helpful advice to individuals and churches confronted by such challenging times: "It is better to be wrong than be silent in the face of problems that are tormenting the thoughts and lives of . . . people. It is easy to explain mistakes for all honest men will understand and sympathize; it is impossible to explain silence, for none will listen."[1]

Once more, there is a time to worship and a time to serve,

a time for spiritual evangelism and a time for social evangelism. How much Christendom has suffered because of a lack of recognition that the two belong together. The people of God will always bear a redemptive witness to those outside the "household of faith." Personal evangelism, soul-winning, must have a high priority in any church. However, such outreach must be followed by programs aimed at bringing maturity to newfound faith or the next generation of Christians will be full grown adults with the spiritual mentality of babies.

Social activists need the power of a worship experience even as contemplatives need the outreach ministry of social action. Without frequent experiences of genuine worship social activists lose not only the ultimate strength needed to do their work, they become somewhat unsure of even what that work is and why it ought to be done. Conversely, unless that which is learned, felt, and experienced in worship is translated into concrete acts of ministry, worship experiences may become little more than a series of self-centered spiritual libations more of the nature of escape from the world than preparation for the world in which discipleship is to be lived out.

For everything there is a season and how important it is that the balance of seasons be maintained.

Study the significance of sensitivity.

Implicit in the Ecclesiastes catalogue of experiences is another important emphasis. Recognition of the seasons of life is not enough in itself. Awareness needs the supplement of wisdom—wisdom which enables a person to discern the nature of the times and to act appropriately.

There is a time to laugh and a time to cry. An individual must not become so involved with either, however, that one without the other becomes a style of life. Jesus recognized this truth. He indicated that while he was present with his disciples a season of fasting and tears was out of order. Yet, he foretold a time when tears would be more appropriate than smiles and when fasting would be more in order than feasting. Such is the wisdom which teaches people not to dance at funerals or mourn at births.

Christians are responsible for developing a sensitivity to the seasons of people's lives that creates opportunities for a helpful response. At various points, ministry in Christ's name may involve us in laughter when we would much prefer to be crying, or in tears when the day otherwise seems more conducive to laughter. Disciples of Christ must never forget the dynamics of either. To the people of God belongs the responsibility of knowing when to listen and when to speak, when to give and when to receive, when to instruct and when to be instructed, when to solemnize and when to celebrate.

Consider how balance may be maintained sensitively.

Growing out of these important insights from Ecclesiastes are two crucial questions. How can such a balance of the seasons be maintained? How can sensitivity to the nature of the seasons be achieved?

In reality, no one can really change the makeup of human experience. In most instances, people are even unable to alter the circumstances which provoke weeping or laughing, silence or conversation. Hope revolves around the possibility of persons being so changed inwardly that they control experiences rather than have experiences control them.

Necessary is the development of what psychologists call a "gyroscopic personality"[2]—the ability of an individual to remain stationary when his or her own environment is revolving. A person who possesses this quality has plumbed the depths of life and discovered that real living does not consist of fluid reactions to each different situation but of a solid commitment to one way of life sufficient for all occasions. Here is truly the "man for all seasons." This person controls situations rather than being controlled by situations.

Syndicated columnist Sydney Harris tells a story which illustrates the point. Harris was accompanying a friend to a newsstand. As the friend greeted the newsman courteously, he received in return gruff and discourteous service. Accepting the newspaper shoved rudely in his direction, the friend politely smiled and wished the newsman a nice weekend. As the two friends walked on, Harris asked, "Does he always treat you so rudely?" The man's response was, "Yes, unfortunately he does." Harris was puzzled and inquired, "And are you always so polite and friendly to him?" The friend said, "Yes, I am." Pressing the issue, Harris asked, "Why are you so nice to him when he is so unfriendly to you?" The friend said (here is the point!), "Because I don't want him to decide how I'm going to act."[3]

Change the characters. Alter the situation. The truth of Harris' friend remains.

Still to be answered is the question of how to develop a sensitivity to each season which can produce a sufficiency for all seasons. This is no innate ability. Obviously, people do not have such power welling up within them. The solution is in what the New Testament describes as redemption—an experience which both transcends and pervades time and all of its experiences.

Paul, for example, could utter the confidence of a man for all seasons only after acceptance of Christ into his life. Following this event, though, he could write: "For I have learned, in whatever state I am, to be content. I know how to be abased, and I know how to abound; in any and all circumstances I have learned the secret of facing plenty and hunger, abundance and want. I can do all things in him who strengthens me" (Phil. 4:11–13). The great apostle bears witness to the fact that life in Christ is the kind of life which permits joy whether one is adorned in a new Hart, Shafner, and Marx suit, a Ruth Von Fierstenberg dress, or a Saturday special from Railroad Salvage. His testimony is that the ups and downs of existence are not dependent upon an invitation to a banquet or the reality of a mealtime without food.

Actually, the Bible sees all of life against the backdrop of this experience called redemption and recognizes that for a person to be fit for any day that person must be "in Christ." Thus, urgency is given to the call to redemption—"now is the acceptable time . . . now is the day of salvation" (2 Cor. 6:2). Christ is the integrative center of life and today is the opportune moment for meeting him.

Even as the cyclical seasons of the year come and go, each individual experiences the seasons of the soul—times of spiritual refreshment as well as times of spiritual aridness, times when life is filled with deep reassuring convictions and times when life is bombarded with doubt, times of weeping and times of laughing, times of celebrating birth and times of grappling with death. That is why it is so important that individuals gain the balance and sensitivity which come only in an encounter with Christ. That is also why now, this ordinary moment, is the most acceptable time to join with him who makes persons sufficient for all seasons.

When life is in Jesus Christ, the words of Ecclesiastes can be read again: "For everything there is a season, and a time for every matter under heaven" (3:1). Now, the immediate response is not mounting anxiety or a gnawing dread but the quietly spoken resolve—"Let the seasons come. Thank God, through Christ, I am ready."

Notes

CHAPTER 2

[1] Sam Keen underscores the significance of this concept in his excellent elaboration on the themes "Exile and Homecoming" in *To a Dancing God* (New York: Harper and Row, 1970), pp. 6–37.

[2] My understanding of this passage in general and these words in particular were aided tremendously by James E. Dittes, *Minister on the Spot* (Philadelphia: Pilgrim Press, 1970), pp. 1–9.

[3] Ibid., p. 7. Dittes writes: *"There is no such thing as being on the verge. It only feels that way. Either be sick where you are, or else there, where you are, 'Take up your pallet and walk.' "*

CHAPTER 3

[1] John W. Gardner, *No Easy Victories,* ed., Helen Rowan (New York: Harper and Row, 1968), p. 32.

[2] The idea of "God's clock" was introduced to this author in a sermon delivered by Dr. George A. Buttrick.

CHAPTER 4

[1] John Henry Jowett, *The Preacher His Life and Work* (New York: Harper and Brothers, 1912), p. 45.

[2] Ibid., p. 50.

[3] C. S. Lewis, *The Screwtape Letters and Screwtape Proposes a Toast* (New York: The Macmillan Company, 1961), p. 10.

CHAPTER 5

[1] Ernst Lohmeyer, *"Our Father": An Introduction to the Lord's Prayer,* trans., John Bowden (New York: Harper and Row, 1965), p. 198.

[2] William Barclay, *The Letters of James and Peter* (Philadelphia: The Westminster Press, 1960), p. 50.